BILLY SUNDAY
Home Run to Heaven

by Robert A. Allen

The White Sox were leading in the ninth with two men already out. The crack as bat met ball could be heard across the entire field. Watching the ball rise, Billy knew it was far over his head. But still he ran. The bleachers, filled beyond capacity, had spilled many of their spectators over into the field. With an eye still on the ball and the crowd parting before him like the Red Sea before Moses, Billy was sure that the ball would go over the fence. Jumping over a bench someone had hauled onto the field, Billy stopped where he thought the ball would come down.

But he had guessed short. It was still going over his head. He jumped as high as he could, shoved his left hand out as far as it could go, and felt the thud as the ball hit his glove. The momentum carried him to the ground, but somehow he held onto the ball.

After the game the other players were on him, pummeling him and cheering him all the way to the clubroom. "Thanks, fellows," said Billy. " But it wasn't just me out there this afternoon. It wasn't just Billy who caught that ball. It was Billy and God."

A pro ballplayer who was also a Christian? No one ever heard of such a thing! But Billy didn't care. Whatever Billy did, he did with total enthusiasm—playing ball and telling people about Jesus.

The first record Billy set in the major leagues was one for the most consecutive strikeouts—thirteen his first thirteen times up to bat. His speed when he finally did start hitting, however, was hard to believe.

ABOUT THE AUTHOR

Robert A. Allen has made a life-long study of the life of Billy Sunday. He says, "During work on a master's degree in speech and theatre arts, I did extensive research and prepared a forty-five minute mono-drama on the life of Billy Sunday. I have presented that recital many times over the last several years." He has also published articles and a play about Billy Sunday.

Mr. Allen, who lives in Missoula, Montana, has four children—Chad, Wendy, Kent, and Tammy.

ABOUT THE ARTIST

Charles Shaw lives in a town with the unlikely name of Dripping Springs, Texas. He especially enjoys drawing pictures that show action and humor. His illustrations have been printed in periodicals as well as in books.

Billy Sunday

Home Run to Heaven

by

Robert A. Allen

Illustrated by Charles Shaw

MOTT MEDIA

Milford, Michigan 48042

COPYRIGHT © 1985 by Mott Media, Inc.

Louise H. Rock, Editor
A. G. Smith, Cover Artist

LIBRARY OF CONGRESS CATALOGING IN PUBLICATION DATA

Allen, Robert A.
    Billy Sunday: Home Run to Heaven

    (The Sowers)
    Bibliography: p. 149
    Includes Index.

    SUMMARY: A biography of a professional baseball player who dedicated his life to spreading the gospel and became one of the most influential religious figures of the early twentieth century.
    1. Sunday, Billy, 1862-1935—Juvenile literature. 2. Evangelists—United States—Biography—Juvenile literature. 3. Baseball players—United States—Biography—Juvenile literature. [1. Sunday, Billy, 1862-1935. 2. Evangelists. 3. Baseball players. 4. Christian biography] I. Shaw, Charles, 1941- ill. II. Title.
BV3785.S8A63   1985   269'.2'0924 [B] [92]   84-60317
ISBN 0-88062-125-7 Paperbound
ISBN 0-88062-124-9 Hardbound

CONTENTS

Preface

Billy Sunday was the first outstanding professional ballplayer to accept Christ and dedicate his life to spreading the gospel. He was one of the most influential religious figures of the first half of this century.

For years I have admired Billy Sunday. I have told people about him and written articles about him. I did extensive research and prepared a forty-five minute mono-drama about his life, which I have presented many times.

It is my hope that this book has captured the excitement of the life Billy Sunday led for Christ, both on the baseball field and in later years. I hope everyone will come to love this man, who has been called the "gymnast for Jesus."

Robert A. Allen

1

Leaving Home

"Ed, wake up! Wake up, Ed! The train is coming."
William Sunday grabbed his older brother's shoulders and shook him hard. As much as he hated the thought of leaving home, he was not about to miss the train which even now he could hear huffing and puffing its way into the depot across the street. Finally, when there was no response, he pulled the pillow out from under the sleeping boy's head and pummeled him with it.

"Hey, what's the big idea," Ed growled, grabbing for the pillow to keep it from hitting him in the face. "Can't a fellow get a little sleep around here?"

"It's the train, Ed. Mom wants us to come now. If we don't hurry we'll be late."

Ed jumped out of bed and pulled on his trousers. The two of them ran out of the little hotel in Ames, Iowa, where they had spent the night, in time to see a huge cloud of smoke roll up from the steam engine as the engineer released the last of the pressure from the boiler and the train screeched to a halt.

"Goodbye, Mom," Ed called back over his shoulder, as he headed for the metal steps the conductor had lifted out of the passenger car and placed on the low depot platform for the convenience of less nimble passengers.

"Goodbye, Mom," echoed William as he stopped in flight to throw his arms around the rapidly aging Mrs. Sunday. And then, so no one could hear, he buried his face in her apron and begged, "I don't want to go to the Orphans' Home. Please take me back to the farm with you."

Nothing would have pleased Mrs. Sunday more than to grant the tearful request of her youngest son. But as much as she wanted to keep the family together, she knew it was impossible. Her oldest son, Roy, was working for board and room on a neighboring farm. But that didn't provide any income for his mother when the wolf of poverty was scratching at the cabin door.

William had been born on November 19, 1862, just four months after his father enlisted as a private in Company E, Twenty-third Iowa Infantry Volunteers. William had been named for his absent soldier father just one month before the elder William Ashley Sunday died of pneumonia while serving his country in Patterson, Missouri, a victim of the War between the States.

It was only through the kindness of William's grandfather, Squire Corey, that Mrs. Sunday had been able to keep the boys at home for even a few years. Many a time Grandfather Corey had stopped by the two-room log cabin the Sundays called home, to leave a few eggs or a freshly butchered chicken. He taught the boys how to shoot the rapidly moving squirrels that scampered through the Iowa forests. He instructed them in the use of the woodshed's axe, and

would have shared with them their father's bricklay-
ing skills except that his tools had been sold long before
to put food on the table. Even Grandfather Corey's
meager income had fallen victim to a poor spring rain
and a scorching hot summer.

Now, with another winter coming on and no way
to feed her growing boys, Mrs. Sunday was doing the
only thing she knew to do—send them to the Soldiers'
Orphans' Home the government had set up in Glenwood for the aid of such families.

Wordlessly she hugged her youngest close and
allowed her tears to mingle with his. Then she wiped
her eyes with a corner of the flour sack apron she wore
over her tattered green crinoline, and turned him in
the direction of the train. Dutifully he scuffed his way
across the platform, up the stairs, and into a seat on
the wooden bench beside Ed.

Ed had deposited their carpetbag containing

everything they owned on the bench. And he had succeeded in lowering one of the wooden windows so they could shout their farewells as the train pulled out of the station. The train rails had been laid across Iowa only three years before, and this was the first train the boys had even seen, much less ridden on. The locomotive began to chug and puff, and the boiler built up a new head of steam. Suddenly the conductor appeared and took hold of the boys by their stiff turned-down collars.

"All right, who opened that window? Those windows weren't made to be opened. What do you think this is, a Pullman car or something? Now get that window back into place before I throw both of you out on the seat of your knickerbockers."

Ed hurriedly slid the frame back up into place.

When the conductor turned to leave, William found his tongue.

"Please, sir, will you tell us when we get to Council Bluffs? We're going to the Soldiers' Orphans' Home at Glenwood, but we have to get off at Council Bluffs. Could you tell us when we get there, sir?"

The conductor turned back with a scowl on his face that soon softened into a half smile when he realized the boys didn't mean any harm.

"Council Bluffs? You'll know, son. That's as far as this here passenger run goes. Have to get to Glenwood some other way from there."

Neither of the boys slept much although it took all that day and the better part of the night to travel the 150 miles from Ames to Council Bluffs. The combination of uneven iron rails and creaking wooden railroad cars made enough noise to keep even the soundest sleeper awake. Besides, the wooden benches with upright backs did not help either. As soon as the train lurched out of one station it was almost time to stop at another junction. About when the sun came up, they managed to catch a few winks, and then the conductor returned.

"Council Bluffs! Council Bluffs! Last stop on this run. Council Bluffs coming up."

Ed was still rubbing his eyes when they climbed off the train, but William had his mind on more important things.

"There's a hotel, Ed!" He pointed across the street. "Let's go get something to eat. I'm hungry!"

Though Ed was older by two years, he was used to following his younger brother's directions. William had a way of taking command, especially in unfamiliar circumstances. Ed had no idea how his brother expected to get food from a hotel when they didn't have even a penny between them. But he knew his brother well enough to follow closely when he started to talk about food.

William marched right up to the front of the hotel and knocked hard on the door. Almost immediately a well-dressed older woman opened it.

"Hello, Ma'am." William was caught in the act of polishing his dusty shoes on the back of his short trousers. "Our names are Ed and Willie Sunday. We're from Ames."

"From Ames?" The hotel woman's hand flew to her mouth in surprise. "You boys haven't run away from home, have you?"

"No, ma'am." Willie shook his head indignantly. "We wouldn't never run away from home. We love our ma. But Pa is dead and we're going to the Soldiers' Orphans' Home at Glenwood." Reaching back toward Ed he pulled a crumpled piece of paper from his brother's pocket. "Here's a letter to Mr. Stephens, the superintendent."

The woman looked at the tear-stained letter, written

by Mrs. Sunday between prayers that had kept her up the entire night before the boys left Ames. Then the woman reached out and gathered both Willie and Ed into her arms.

"My husband was a soldier, and he never came back either. He wouldn't turn anyone away, and I certainly wouldn't turn you boys away."

That was just what William and Ed had been waiting for. Those buckwheat cakes and sage-spiced sausages really tasted good! They ate until their stomachs bulged. Then, since it was so quiet compared to the train, they lay down in front of the fireplace and slept until noon.

After another big meal, they strolled over to the Burlington Railroad yards, trying to figure out how to get to Glenwood without walking twenty miles. A freight train was being assembled that looked as if it might be headed in the right direction. Following Willie's lead again, the two brothers climbed on the caboose. Men shouted at each other up and down the rails as the couplings were noisily connected, but no one looked in the caboose until the train was underway and the brakeman swung aboard.

"Hey, what are you fellows doing in here? This ain't no passenger train."

Willie hung his head and scuffed his foot on the worn floorboards. "We ain't got no tickets, sir," he said in his most helpless-sounding voice. "We ain't got no money, either. But we sure do need a ride to Glenwood."

"Glenwood!" the brakeman exploded. "That's twenty miles from here. It's too late to throw you off now, but you'll have to get off at Pacific Junction, our first stop."

"Pacific Junction!" The tears began to well up in

Willie's eyes. Ed was pretty sure they were fake and he hoped the brakeman wouldn't realize that.

"We've got to get to Glenwood, sir. We're going to the Soldiers' Orhpans' Home. Our pa is dead." As he spoke, Willie looked out the side of his eye to see how the story was affecting the man who had the power to make them walk the last twenty miles, as their ma had intended. The expression on the man's face told him he was getting somewhere, so he brought out his clincher—the letter their ma had written. It was now crumpled in his own pocket where he had stuffed it after showing it to the woman at the hotel.

"Here's our letter of introduction to Mr. Stephens, the superintendent."

The brakeman smoothed out the crumpled sheet on the table in front of him and squinted to make out the small, tear-blotted writing.

"Dear Squire," he read aloud, "these boys are the only thing I have left in the world. Please take good care of them. Their father served with Company E, Twenty-third Iowa Infantry Volunteers, and has been gone these ten years. Make my boys mind, and God bless you." When he finished reading, a tear from his own eye escaped and further stained Mrs. Sunday's letter.

"It's all right, boys. I'll take you to Glenwood. It won't cost you a cent to ride my train."

2

The Soldiers' Orphanage

In spite of loneliness, Ed and Billy (as the other boys insisted on calling him) grew to like the orphans' home at Glenwood. There were always other boys to play with, and Mr. and Mrs. Stephens were kind even if they were very strict.

Most of the rules didn't bother the boys. They were used to obeying their ma and doing chores. But one thing they had never learned back on the farm was how to watch a clock and be on time. When they had wandered through the woods with their dog, Watch, at their heels they hadn't much cared what time it was. It was only after a squirrel on the limb above chattered defiantly and the gun cracked in reply, bringing the squirrel down at their feet, that they would remember their hunger and run home to receive both a meal and compliments for their skill as marksmen.

But it was not that way at Glenwood. The day was completely scheduled. If a boy was late arriving for a meal, he had to miss the next one as punishment. Billy would often wander out to the far edges of the orphanage property to think about the farm, or get involved in a game of mumbletypeg which couldn't be interrupted even for eating.

Finally Billy became so skinny that Ed decided it was time to do something about it.

"I've volunteered for kitchen duty every night this month," he informed his brother one day when Billy had eaten only two meals in the last six served.

"Whatever for? That's the silliest thing I've heard in a long time."

Being assigned to chores was one thing, but volunteering for them was another!

Ed just grinned and pulled Billy closer as he whispered in his ear. "You be there when I lock up tonight and see if you can't get locked in by mistake. Then I'll discover the mistake in fifteen minutes or so and come back to let you out."

So it was that the pantry at the Orphans' Home was raided repeatedly all during the time the Sunday boys were housed there. Billy never took more than he could eat, but even so he could make a real hole in the supplies during those fifteen minutes before Ed "discovered" his mistake. So Billy never did learn to be on time, and Mr. and Mrs. Stephens noticed he stayed active and cheerful even when he missed so many meals.

The boys had been at Glenwood a little over a year, when the Glenwood Home was discontinued and everyone was moved to a new home in Davenport, Iowa, including the Stephenses, who were to serve as teachers in the larger school. The superintendent of the Davenport Home, Mr. S.W. Pierce, came to travel with the children to their new location.

The train ride seemed almost familiar this time, but

as they rode along through the Iowa countryside Billy came to a conclusion.

"Ed," he whispered to his brother, who was sitting by the window. "I've had enough of orphanages."

"What do you mean?"

"I mean I want to go home. We could both work and help support Ma. We could make it, I know we could."

"But we aren't going to Ames."

"We're going to Des Moines. That's only about thirty miles from home. And I've decided. When we get to Des Moines I'm going to jump the train. I'll be home before morning. How about it? Want to come with me?"

Ed turned away from the window and his eyes widened. He didn't say yes or no to Billy's plan. In fact, he didn't say anything at all. He just stared. Billy, thinking Ed was caught by surprise with the plan, pushed a little harder.

"I know you're having trouble with that leg, but we can make it. Won't it be great to see Ma again, and Watch, and Squire Corey, and all the guys?"

Something desperate in Ed's face finally convinced Billy that Ed was not thinking about Billy's plan at all. Slowly Billy swung around in his seat to see where Ed was staring. He found himself face to face with Mr. Pierce.

"Oh, hello, Mr. Pierce." Billy thought frantically, trying to recall what he had said since the glazed look of recognition had first come over his brother's face. "Are we getting close to Des Moines, sir?"

"That we are, son." Mr. Pierce smiled a mysterious smile that gave Billy no idea concerning how much he had heard. "Is that where you and your brother are from?"

Billy glanced at Ed, who was already shaking his head vigorously. He decided that maybe Mr. Pierce hadn't heard much. "No, sir," he replied. "We're from Ames."

"Tell me," Mr. Pierce continued, "did you like it at Glenwood?"

Both boys nodded without hesitation. "Yes, sir," said Billy. "We liked it at Glenwood real much, sir."

For a time Mr. Pierce stared out the window. Billy, doing the same, realized that the train was slowing down for its stop in Des Moines.

"Well, here's Des Moines," he blurted out. "Do you suppose you had better go check on the engineer, sir?"

The superintendent made no move to take his suggestion. He simply stood by the bench until the train started up again and chugged its way out of the Des Moines depot. Then he smiled his mysterious smile and asked another question.

"Do you boys think that you will like it at Davenport?"

Billy turned toward the bench in front of him and scowled so Mr. Pierce couldn't see. "Yes, sir," he mumbled. "I'm sure we'll enjoy our stay at Davenport real much, sir."

Davenport was a lot like Glenwood in many ways, but the Stephenses had nothing on Mr. Pierce when it came to making rules. Each boy had a long list of things he had to do every day. Anyone who missed even one item on his list received demerits.

"Not cleaning face," Billy read to his brother as they were settling into their room for the first day. "Three demerits.

"Hair uncombed, three demerits.

"Not making bed, eight demerits.

"I'll never get used to all these rules," he complained.

And he didn't. None of them seemed to make any practical sense, especially the requirement that they memorize a Bible verse every day. More than once Billy's school grades were lowered because he had too many demerits for not learning his verses.

One thing he did enjoy, however, was the chore to which he was assigned. Scrubbing floors became his "long suit" and there was not a fellow in the place who could measure up to him in that. He also enjoyed the athletic games that were played every Saturday afternoon. Foot racing and baseball were his favorites, as he was far and away the fastest runner at the home.

About a year after they arrived at Davenport, Ed had a birthday and was suddenly too old to stay at the orphanage any more. Billy was not about to stay by himself. So both boys caught a train and headed home in spite of Mr. Pierce's insistence that Billy stay. Two years away from the woods had been enough for him .

What a reunion they had! The log cabin outside of Ames had not changed a bit. Their ma was older and grayer, but she was so glad to see them that she did nothing but cry for the first two hours. And then she insisted that they all get down on their knees before the old family Bible, read it, and pray for what seemed to Billy like another hour.

The boys stayed at home for a couple of days, then were off to Nevada, Iowa, to look for work.

Billy's first job was as a janitor in a school in Nevada. He had to get up at two o'clock in the morning and carry coal to the fourteen stoves in the building. Then he started all fourteen fires and kept them going throughout the day until all the teachers left in the evening. After that he swept the floors so the building would be ready for the next day. Finally

he was free to go home to study for the classes he managed to attend between his other duties.

The schools in Glenwood and Davenport had done a good job in giving the boys their elementary education. In Nevada, when Billy turned fourteen, he was ready to go on to the secondary school.

His favorite subjects were geography, history, and civil government—that is, until he signed up for a class in elocution. Most of the kids dreaded elocution class and hated to get up in front of everyone to give speeches, but not Billy. To him it was almost as exciting as standing up to the plate with a bat. The teacher gave them speeches to memorize, then instructed them in how to say each word and what to do with their hands while they were saying it.

Every hand movement had a particular meaning which they were taught right along with the words. If you held out your hands with the palms up, that meant approval. If you balled up your fist, that expressed anger. Billy's teacher claimed that if you were good enough with your hand and body movements, you wouldn't have to say anything. People could still tell what you were thinking. Billy loved it.

Oftentimes, as Billy carried the coal for the stoves in the morning, he shouted his favorite speeches at the top of his lungs, gesturing widely with the coal bucket, shovel, or whatever else was handy.

"Ye call me chief," he would shout, imitating Spartacus as he challenged the gladiators in the Roman arena. "And ye do well to call me chief." Suddenly his hands would fly up in the gesture of approval, and whatever he was carrying would fly up with it. Almost every ceiling in the school had mysterious black marks on it, caused by the flying coal when Billy practiced his speech-making.

Billy's salary for the janitor work was twenty-five

dollars a month. Each time he received his check he would take it down to the bank to cash it and take it home to the log cabin for Ma. Ed did the same with his check and Roy occasionally sent a few dollars back from Des Monies where he had found a paying job. It wasn't a lot, but it made life a little easier for their ma.

One day he pushed his check in under the teller's window and forty dollars was pushed back instead of twenty-five. He didn't discover the mistake until he had left the bank. He knew his check had been for only twenty-five dollars. But instead of going back into the bank, he decided to talk to a lawyer friend of his.

"Frank, what do you think? Jay King handed me forty dollars and my check only called for twenty-five."

The lawyer whistled and then laughed. "Billy, if I had your luck I would buy a lottery ticket."

"But the fifteen dollars isn't mine, is it?" Billy persisted.

"It certainly is. Don't be a chump. If you were shy ten dollars and you went back, they wouldn't give it to you, would they? And if they hand out fifteen dollars, don't be a fool. Keep it!"

Billy still wasn't sure, but his friend was a lawyer. So that week Ma received her twenty-five dollars and Billy became the owner of his first store-bought clothes. The pants were brown with little green flecks in them, and the shirt had been sewn on a machine. Billy thought he was the goods when he had on his store clothes.

The rest of the money was blown on something that would have broken his mother's heart if she had known. He spent it on what everyone called "booze." All of the high school fellows drank once in a while.

And now that Billy had some money, they expected him to buy. So he did.

There was only one problem. Every time his mother would get them down on their knees beside the Bible to pray, Billy would hear a voice inside him saying, "Fifteen dollars with interest, Nevada County, Iowa; fifteen dollars, Bill."

"Lord, the bank don't know I got that fifteen dollars," he would say to himself.

But the voice would come again, "Bill, you owe that Farmers' Bank fifteen dollars with interest."

Finally, since the only time it bothered him was when his mother was praying, Billy decided that he would just stay away from the praying.

He could tell it hurt Ma, but never again as long as he was home did Billy join the little prayer circle around the family Bible.

3

Independence Day

Fifteen-year-old Billy Sunday sat straight up in bed. Outside his window the boom of a cannon still echoed through the early morning mist. It was the Fourth of July and the cannon on the grounds of nearby Iowa State College signaled the beginning of the nation's birthday celebration.

Before the echo of the big gun died out in the corn fields, Billy jumped into his denims and sprinted out to the shed to milk the cows. The pails were filled in record time and he lugged them into the house quickly, but carefully, so as not to slop cream over the sides.

"It's Independence Day, Ma. Will you be joining us in town for the big celebration?"

Mrs. Sunday took the buckets from her youngest son and set them in the little ice box. The ice would last just long enough to keep the milk cool until she could separate it and make her butter. "Maybe later, Billy. But don't you wait for me. Just eat a bite of breakfast and run along."

Five minutes, six pancakes, and two glasses of milk later, Billy was racing down the road in the direction of Marshalltown, Iowa.

The streets were already starting to fill up with people at 6:30 in the morning. Along Main Street men were busy setting up refreshment stands where lemonade, sweet crackers, bologna, ice cream, and dill pickles would be offered in exchange for sticky nickels and pennies clutched tightly in grubby fingers. Other men were erecting makeshift booths with huge signs over them which read:

Fireworks 10¢

Billy made his way down to the far end of Main Street where a tall spire crowned a low hill. On the side of the spire was a metal plaque, and Billy searched as he had so many times before for the familiar name. It was listed under Company E, Twenty-third Iowa Infantry Volunteers. William Ashley Sunday, PFC,

1862. The tall war memorial to the dedicated soldiers of the Civil War was the closest Billy had ever come to his father.

This was a day to honor those who had given their lives for their country, but Billy couldn't stay at the memorial for long. There was too much going on around him.

"Hey, Billy. Over here!"

Racing down the street toward him were five boys of various sizes, ages, and shapes, but all dressed in the same brown shirts and short pants. They were from the Soldiers' Orphanage, and Billy knew them well.

"Hiya, fellows! So Mr. Stephens decided to let you come this year."

"That's just 'cause you weren't there to spoil it with your tricks. He's like to never forget how you got yourself locked into the commissary so you could eat all you wanted."

"He's still not sure it was me," Billy defended himself as they headed out toward the fairgrounds.

"No, but he's pretty sure. It hasn't happened again since you left."

"Well, I'll tell you this!" Billy laughed. "I never ate that well before. And probably never will again."

At the fairgrounds, workers were setting up tables for the picnic dinner later in the day. And they were also registering folks for competition in shooting and racing.

"You gonna run this year, Billy?" The questioner was "Skinny," one of the boys from the home, and the fastest of them all. "There's a silver dollar for the winner."

"Nah. Don't think so."

"Why not? You can beat all of us fellows in a hundred yards."

"I've been thinking about entering the free-for-all instead. There's three dollars resting on that one."

"But that's against the men, Billy!"

The boys watched in amazement as Billy walked up to the amusements committee table and boldly signed his name on the free-for-all race list.

"Now, let's go back to town and 'blow' some money."

None of the boys had much of that, but they made what they had go a long way. Three cents' worth of sweet crackers, ten cents' worth of bologna, and a dish of ice cream for a nickel. That made them thirsty.

"Right this way, ladies and gentlemen!" the barkers were calling. "Ice-cold lemonade, made in the shade, stirred with a spade—step right this way. Only five cents, one-half of a dime." So each of the boys had a glass of lemonade, and then they were broke.

About two o'clock, it was time for the big race. In addition to Billy, thirteen men had signed up.

"All right, fellows. You know the rules. One hundred yards straight out. Prize, three dollars."

The starter was a tall man with long whiskers who had once been the mayor. The fourteen racers lined up at the starting point with Billy at the far end. His buddies from the Orphans' Home crowded through the other spectators to get a better look.

"Come on, Billy! Let's have one for the country boys!"

Right next to Billy was a professor from Iowa State College with real running shoes and a rose-colored sweat outfit. Billy's outfit was the same blue denim he had been wearing all day.

"On your marks!"

Billy propped his right foot against the log which lay behind the starting line to serve as a booster for the runners.

"Get set!"

Next to him, the professor leaned over and placed both hands on the ground, crouching down for the fastest sprint possible. Billy just leaned forward and set his teeth as if they had lockjaw. His fists were clenched and he was breathing as if he had already run the race.

From way off near the finish line he heard a voice he was sure was his grandpa's calling, "Go it, son! Go it!" And then the entire crowd was jumping and shrieking as the man in the whiskers shouted "Go!"

The professor took off like a scared jack-rabbit and beat Billy off the log, but within ten yards they were neck and neck and pulling ahead of the pack. The only other runner keeping up with them was a long-legged farmer named Bates. At fifty yards it was definitely a race between the three of them, and the crowd went wild.

"Go it, Bill, go it!" shouted the boys from the orphanage.

"Go for State!" the college crowd was chanting on the other side.

No one at all seemed to be rooting for Bates, and at seventy-five yards he dropped behind. Billy and the spiffy-dressed professor were still side by side and stride for stride. The professor's legs were longer, but Billy was running like a colt on the first day's breaking. His sides ached and his legs were starting to feel as if they were running by themselves instead of being attached to his body. He pushed them down extra hard, but still he could hear the professor's raspy breath right behind him, sounding like the steam calliope that led the parade when the circus came to town.

With just five feet to go Billy lunged forward and crossed the finish line first. Immediately he was swarmed by his buddies from the orphanage.

"Bring on your college professors," they chanted as they lifted him up on their shoulders. "We can beat the whole bunch."

As a gang they rushed uptown to collect the winnings from a merchant named Soper. With the victor in the lead they burst open the door of his general store and charged in.

"Mr. Soper? I've come to collect my winnings. Give me my three dollars for winning the foot race."

"Ah go on!" The merchant didn't even turn around from placing bottles of sarsaparilla on the shelf. "That was a man's race. The boys' race will come later on." Pierce

"But he won it, Mr. Soper. We all saw him do it."

"It was a free-for-all, sir. And I even beat the college professor."

Mr. Soper turned around then and smiled indulgently at the hayseedy mob which had invaded his store. "Sure you did, boy. Why, he's been running for years, in lots of races. Do you expect me to believe that?"

"But it's the truth, sir. All the fellows here will tell you the same thing."

But the more they talked the more Mr. Soper refused to hand over the prize money. It began to look as if Billy was going to win the race and still not earn the reward when the man with the whiskers came into the store.

"Missed a great race, Soper. This boy here won the free-for-all. Beat the college professor by a good three feet, I suppose."

Without a word Mr. Soper reached under the counter and pulled out three silver dollars. For the next few minutes there was such whooping and hollering that some people out in the street thought the fireworks had begun already—inside Mr. Soper's General Store.

"Come on, boys. Lemonade and ice cream on me." Billy led the whole gang back out into the street and down to the refreshment stands. For the next few hours he was a millionaire.

Late that afternoon the boys from the orphanage headed back with Mr. Stephens, and Billy started home. As he trudged down Main Street, he was thinking about the race when he almost ran into a man standing in front of the news office.

"Are you William Sunday?" He was a tall man and wore what Billy thought must have been at least a thirty-dollar suit.

"Yes sir, that's me." Even as he said it, the man stuck out his hand and Billy grabbed it in a firm handshake.

"Name's McFarland, Charles McFarland. *Times-Republican.*"

"Pleased to meet you, sir." Billy knew then that it was an expensive suit the man wore. Mr. McFarland was editor and publisher of the largest circulation newspaper in the entire county.

"Hear you won the foot race today, young man."

Billy just nodded. Asking Mr. Soper for his winnings with all the fellows around had been one thing. But trying to put words together to say to one of the wealthiest men in town was another.

"Listen, son. Some of the businessmen here in Marshalltown have been putting up some money to get a first-rate baseball team going. I realize you're still a little young for this sort of thing—but the way you can run, well, we sure could use a runner like that out in left field. How about it? Are you interested in playing baseball?"

4

Championship Game

The next four summers spelled baseball for Billy. During the winter he worked to help out Ma, spent some weeks in school when work wasn't readily available, and dreamed about baseball. In the summers his dreams came true.

The summer of the year he was nineteen the team from Marshalltown had played almost every team in the state and had not lost a game. The papers, especially Mr. McFarland's *Times-Republican*, were saying they had the best baseball team in the entire state. But the Des Moines papers disagreed.

"Listen to this, team!" The players were all gathered in the clubhouse dressing for practice when the manager rushed in waving a copy of the Des Moines paper. "The businessmen in Des Moines have raised five hundred dollars for a championship game. They are calling for five hundred from each team plus gate money for the winner. And they want to play us!"

"I hear they've got some powerful right-handers," spoke up the catcher.

"Nothing we can't handle," responded the manager. "Why, we've got Billy out in left field, and he can catch anything as long as it stays inside the park."

"Where will we get the money?"

"I can answer that." Everyone turned to look at the door, from where the voice was coming. There stood Mr. McFarland, beaming from ear to ear. "I met with some other businessmen this morning, as soon as we saw the paper. The five hundred dollars has already been pledged, plus train fare for the entire team down to Des Moines and back. We're counting on you fellows to capture that championship for Marshalltown, and we believe you can do it."

"Three cheers for Mr. McFarland," called the manager, and for the next few minutes there was as much shouting and cheering in the clubhouse as if they had already won the game.

The championship game was to be played in Des Moines. It seemed as if everyone from Marshalltown was on the train that carried them down for the game. Someone said the Rock Island Railroad had added six extra cars just to carry everyone who had purchased tickets. But when all those people moved into the stadium they were still a small group compared to the hometown crowd. It was the largest stadium Billy had ever seen, much less played ball in.

Billy and his teammates dressed quietly that day, somewhat awed by the beautiful facilities and the amount of money resting on their success or failure. But at the same time they spoke confidently of what they would do to the home team.

"Three runs. I think we'll beat them by three

runs.'' The catcher slugged his fist deep into his big mitt to emphasize the point.

"Games aren't won until the last inning," the manager warned.

"Don't forget their power sluggers," added the relief pitcher.

"Don't forget our power fielder," retorted the catcher. "By the way, Billy, have you heard who's going to be in the bleachers this afternoon?"

"Not a word, Mutt." Billy picked up his glove and headed for the field, anxious for the game to get underway.

"Well, I heard tell that Aunt Em was going to bring her nephew along."

"So what! Does the kid want an autograph or something?"

"Aunt Em's nephew is no kid. He's 'Pop' Anson."

Billy slid to a stop halfway out the door, like a base runner trapped between third and home. "*The* Pop Anson? Captain A.C. Anson of the Chicago White Stockings?"

Mutt nodded gleefully. "The same. Aunt Em has been telling him about you for years, but he always comes to visit her in the winter when we're not playing. So when the championship game was announced she wrote him and—"

"What are we waiting for?" Billy shouted. "Let's get out there and run those guys out of the ballpark."

With a howl that echoed off the far side of the bleachers and brought a corresponding shriek for the Marshalltown fans, the entire team burst onto the field, ready for the game—and Pop Anson.

Billy Sunday was not a great hitter, but he could stretch any hit he did get into additional bases. His first time up he lined one into center field for what should have been a one-bagger, but by the time the

center fielder had the ball back into the infield, Billy
had gone around first and into second on a stand-up
double. The next time he came to bat he hit a short
grounder and should have been thrown out at first.
But the first baseman remembered the speed with
which he had rounded the bases the first time.

"Hurry it up! Hurry it up!" he yelled to the right
fielder, who was handling the grounder.

"I've got it," called back the fielder. Hurrying to
pick it up he fired it hard at the first baseman. In his
hurry he threw it wide, and his teammate had to reach
for it—right in the path of Billy who was coming down
from home like greased lightning. All that the crowd
could see was the cloud of dust as the entire play
exploded in mid-air. When the dust settled, the ball
was rolling on the ground and Billy was safe on first.
Before the third inning was over he had stolen three
bases, caught four flies, and scored twice. The Marshalltown team was leading 6-5.

As Billy stood out in the field while the home team
was up to bat, his attention was riveted on the batter. He watched him like a snake, swaying from side
to side as the batter adjusted his stance. He mentally
calculated every move, and after a batter had been
up one time, Billy had a pretty good idea where that
man would hit the ball. They had some powerful hitters, all right, but Billy's speed put him underneath
almost every long ball they hit.

When Billy was on the bench waiting for his turn
in the line-up, he took a little time to think about the
fact that Captain "Pop" Anson was in the stands.
A.C. Anson had been the first player to make more
than three thousand base hits during a career. He was
just about the most famous man in baseball except
maybe Old Hoss Radbourn. Anson was the player-
coach of the famous Chicago White Stockings and had

a reputation for discovering young talent. Billy had never before dreamed of having a career in baseball, but he was dreaming today.

The eighth inning came, and it looked as if the Des Moines businessmen were out five hundred dollars. The Marshalltown team had increased their lead to four runs. The score stood nine to five, local hopes were fading fast. But then the first man up popped a short infield fly which the second baseman bobbled, and made it to first. Two batters later the bases were loaded and the tying run was at the plate. And worst of all, Des Moines was at the top of their batting order.

Billy dug his heels into the dirt and leaned forward, ready for the long hit he was certain would come. The Marshalltown pitcher stretched and pitched his change-up, a slow blooper that drifted lazily in toward the plate. The Des Moines slugger started to swing, expecting a fast ball, then checked himself and swung again, popping a high fly just behind the shortstop. Billy had been all primed for the long fly, but he recovered quickly and charged toward the infield. The runner on third hesitated, not sure whether the fleet-footed fielder could actually reach the fly. But before Billy could get there the ball dropped out of the sky and bounced crazily. The man on third was sliding into home when Billy's shotgun throw arrived.

"Safe!" roared the umpire behind second.

One run was in, the bases were still loaded, the tying run was on first, and the big hitters were still to come. The fans from Des Moines stamped their feet on the wooden bleachers and chanted in rhythm, "Home run! Home run! Home run!"

There was no time to think about the missed fly ball as Billy raced back deep into left field to get set for the next pitch. This time the pitcher ran the count

to three and two before releasing one of his favorite fast balls.

"Crack!" From the sound that reached him in deep left Billy knew the hitter had connected solidly with the ball. The ball still seemed to be rising as he raced toward deep left. The fence grew larger and larger, but all Billy could think about was the ball and the loaded bases. At the last possible minute he leaped, using the fence as a vault, and snatched the ball from the air. The third base runner, certain that the ball was long gone, had already sprinted for home.

"Go back," yelled the coach.

"Third base, Billy," yelled the Marshalltown fans.

Sunday saw at a glance the entire situation and fired an impossible long bomb from where he had landed. The runner made it back to third just as the ball came steaming into the glove of the third baseman. He was safe, but one man was out and no additional runs had scored.

"Go it, Bill. Go it!" roared the fans. The young left fielder raised his hands above his head in response before settling in for the next play of the game.

Billy's impossible catch fired up his teammates. The pitcher struck out the next batter with four pitches. The next man up was the best batter Des Moines had, but he tried to pull it into right field to keep it away from Billy. He succeeded only in popping a blooper which the fielder handled easily. The side was retired with the bases loaded and only one run. The rally had failed.

In the top of the ninth, Billy was the first man up to bat. He strode up to the plate to the tune of cheers from the Marshalltown bleachers, doffed his hat to the crowd, and let the first pitch go by.

"Strike one!" bellowed the umpire.

Billy just grinned and stepped out of the batter's box to spit on his hands. He got set for the next pitch and it whizzed past him. The pitcher was determined to pay him back for his catch by striking him out.

"Strike two!" the umpire shouted.

This time Billy stayed in the box and ground his left foot down into the dirt. The Des Moines pitcher stretched, and threw. The move was the same, but Billy spotted it immediately for what it was—the change of pace pitch, a lazy curve. Taking a quick half step backward he slid his right hand up on the bat about eight inches and bunted. The ball flew about fifteen feet toward the shortstop and landed right in the middle of three players who were all trying to field it. By the time the pitcher and the third baseman let the shortstop have it, Billy was well on his way to first.

But to everyone's surprise he didn't stop there. Feet pounding, he rounded first without even pausing and headed down the second base line. The first baseman, thinking Billy had turned the wrong way, reached out to tag him. But Billy wasn't turning at all—he was using his bunt for a two bagger. Recovering quickly, the first basemen fired the ball toward second base, right over Billy's head. The second baseman, still in the infield where the bunt had landed, raced back to cover his base and catch the ball.

It looked as if Billy would be out on second. But nearly ten feet from second he left his feet and propelled himself toward second base in a headlong slide. The dust rolled. The ball came sizzling in, high enough to miss the runner's head had he been standing up, and high enough that the second baseman who was already on the plate had to jump slightly to catch it. It was during that small jump that Billy's outstretched hand reached the base. He had beat the throw.

The umpire tried to yell ''Safe,'' but no one was listening. In the Marshalltown bleachers, the fans were screaming their throats raw, hugging each other, and jumping on their neighbors' feet. On the other side of the stadium they were roaring just as loud in total disbelief. And the one who had caused all the ruckus was standing on second base, casually wiping the dirt from his uniform. The next batter hit a home run, but you would have thought Billy had hit it by the ovation they gave him as he crossed home plate. By the end of that last inning the score was fifteen to six in favor of Marshalltown, and the championship was theirs. Billy had scored six times and made eight putouts himself.

It took nearly two hours for the team to make their way to the dressing room after the game. They had to shake hands with everyone once and with all the youngsters several times. Billy kept glancing around for someone that fit his idea of what the manager of a championship baseball team looked like, but no one showed up. Finally the catcher, Mutt, came up with a spry-looking elderly lady who was smiling so big you would have thought she won the game herself.

"Billy, I want you to meet Aunt Em."

"So this is the young man with the locomotive legs. I've been watching you for several years, Billy. And I think you're ready for the big leagues. If only my nephew 'Cap' could have been here today."

"You mean he didn't make it?" Billy tried to hide his disappointment.

"No, son. Got tied up in Chicago and missed his train. But I'm going to tell him all about it, you can bet your bottom dollar on that. And when I get done telling him about this game, you're going to hear from the Chicago White Stockings, mark my word."

5

Play Ball

"A.G. Spaulding's Sporting Goods Store." Billy read the sign over the door of the large building in downtown Chicago and then looked again at the telegram he carried in his pocket. "That's where the telegram said to come," he said to no one in particular.

He had arrived in the "windy city" late the previous night. With only one dollar in his pocket he could not afford a room, so the depot of the Burlington Northern had served as a bedroom. Seven o'clock found him in front of Spaulding's store, but no one else was around. It was not until eight o'clock that a clerk finally arrived.

"Excuse me, sir!" Billy jumped up from the curb. "I have a telegram here from Cap Anson telling me to meet him here at Mr. Spaulding's store. Can you tell me where to find him?"

The clerk eyed him in disbelief. Billy thought of the picture he must present—his hair was long, with ragged edges where his mother had clipped it with the shears. The clerk's hair was short and tapered, obviously shaped by a big-city barber. Billy had no hat, collar, or tie, while the clerk sported a tall top-hat, a turn-down stiff starched collar, and a ready-made bow tie.

"Cap'n Anson?" The clerk pushed past the young ballplayer, obviously not wanting to be bothered with such a ragamuffin. "Just wait and he'll come."

So Billy waited. About ten o'clock some of the ballplayers started showing up. Compared to them, Billy felt like a long-haired hayseed from the Iowa cornfields. He had just about decided to turn tail and run when Captain A.C. Anson arrived. Anson was six-feet-two, square-shouldered, and tightly muscled, with a nose that bent like a fishing hook. Since boyhood, Billy had admired this man, under whose leadership the White Stockings had won five league pennants in six years. Though Billy was usually not at a loss for words, the very sight of Cap Anson tied his tongue up in knots.

"Hello, Cap'n Anson." Billy scuffed his feet nervously. "I, uh, got your telegram. And, well, here I am."

The captain didn't seem to notice that Billy was ill at ease. Everything with him was strictly business.

"Glad you made it, Sunday. If you're half as good a player as my Aunt Em claims, we'll be in business. I hear you're a pretty good runner."

"Well, I don't know. I have done some running."

"Good. Fred Pfeffer's our crack runner now. Let's go over to the ballpark and see how you stack up against him in a race."

That was fine with Billy. Anything was better than standing around getting sized up under the gaze of pro ballplayers like Mike Kelly and John Clarkson. Besides, a race would let them size him up in style.

Half an hour later they were in the locker room of a stadium that made the one in Des Moines look like a sand-lot.

Larry Cochrane offered him a uniform and shoes, but no one wore Billy's size. So he just took off his boots and prepared to run barefoot against Pfeffer.

"Go!" Cap yelled, and they were off. From the first it was obvious that the new recruit was fast. By the time they rounded first base he led by five feet. Billy increased his lead down the second base line, but rounding second he caught a bare toe on the bag and went sprawling. Pfeffer pounded past, and Billy sprung to his feet in dismay, certain that the race was lost. Desperation fueled his mad dash around third. As they crossed home plate he pulled ahead once more to win the race.

"You really got speed, boy, and that's one thing every team can use. If you can field and hit, we can sure find a place for you on this team."

Billy had never had trouble with either fielding or hitting. But then he had never faced professional pitchers before either. The first record he set in the major leagues was one for the most consecutive strikeouts—thirteen his first thirteen times up to bat. His speed when he finally did start hitting, however, justified Aunt Em's recommendation. Many a ball was thrown away at first simply because the opposing teams knew they had to hurry to beat him to the base. His record of ninety-five bases stolen in one year stood until 1915 when it was broken by the great Ty Cobb. And he was the first man in professional baseball to round the bases in less than fourteen seconds.

Those were the days when baseball traditions were being established and the rules were still being written. A.G. Spaulding, who owned the Chicago team, had been the first player to wear an obvious baseball glove. Even catchers had caught barehanded in previous years. Frank Flint, the Chicago catcher, had broken every bone in the ball of his hand at one time or another, plus many in his face. He caught for years without a chest protector, mask, or glove.

Alexander Cartwright had written down many of the rules by which baseball in Billy's day was played when he organized his Knickerbocker Base Ball Club in New York in 1845. But changes were being made every year as the game developed.

During Billy's years with the White Stockings, the pitching distance was increased from forty-five to fifty feet. And it would be increased again just after he left baseball to the present sixty feet, six inches. Part of the change was due to the amazing speed of Charlie (Old Hoss) Radbourn who in 1884 pitched seventy-three complete games and won sixty of them. At forty-five feet he was almost impossible to hit off of.

A major change in pitching also took place during those years. The professional leagues agreed in 1884 to allow pitchers to pitch overhanded. Up to that time the game had been played with underhanded pitching and the new speed, which came as a part of the switch, was another reason for the change in pitching distance.

One of Billy's favorite tricks because of his great speed was to catch a foul ball on the first bounce when he was playing right or left field. Until 1883 that was still considered an out. But they changed the rule that year so that no fly ball was an out unless caught before it bounced.

Part of the reason for Billy's strikeout record— thirteen whiffs his first thirteen times at bat— was because called strikes had only became a part of the game in 1868. Before that a batter only made strikes by swinging and missing. They could let as many balls go by as they wished. Even when Billy joined the White Stockings, batters didn't walk until after nine balls. The nine-ball-walk rule was a hot one for debate until 1889 when the present four-ball rule was introduced.

Many of the players excelled at a number of field positions. The "star" of the team, Mike "King" Kelly, played catcher, first, second, third, shortstop, and even pitched successfully. But he was best known for his daring steals. He would slide into base feet first, hands first, or even with a slide and a flip if he thought that would keep him away from the glove of the opponent. Every time he left a base the crowd would get excited and start to chant, "Slide, Kelly, slide."

When he came to third base, Kelly would watch over his shoulder to see where the only umpire was looking. Should the umpire be watching to see if the ball was a fair one, Kelly would cut suddenly toward the plate, right past the pitcher's mound, and pound into home without ever coming within fifteen feet of third base.

Of course, the third baseman would scream bloody murder, but the home crowd would drown him out. More than once an umpire who was not on his toes was left to harbor angry suspicions about Mike Kelly.

Kelly made no secret of the fact that he was a heavy drinker. He enjoyed being a hero and a big spender. His fine Irish face with its red mustache and fiery eyes graced many billboards, advertising everything from streetcars to cigars. Every boy in America idolized him, and Billy, at twenty years of age, was still enough of a boy to do the same. It was not long before Billy was joining the rest of the team in the saloons on their nights off.

Though all of the players drank, most of them knew enough not to drink when it would affect their game. They knew Captain Anson wouldn't put up with that. The team was in the running for championship honors every year and nothing was allowed to interfere.

Between Spaulding and Anson, the Chicago team had developed into the best-known ball club in the nation. They were the first to go south for spring training and the first to take an all-star team on a tour around the world.

Billy Sunday loved baseball and played it with total enthusiasm. The team was successful year after year, and he was making good money. And then came the championship game of 1886.

The previous year, the two most famous teams in the country, the Chicago White Stockings and the St. Louis Browns, had engaged in a series of games marked by squabbles which had settled nothing as far as a world championship was concerned. In fact, both sides claimed the prize because one game had been awarded to Chicago by forfeit on decision of the umpire.

But 1886 was different. The Browns had already won the championship of the American Association and Mr. Spaulding had accepted their challenge to a World Championship Series on a "winner-take-all" basis. Fifteen thousand dollars rested on the outcome of the series—the largest purse ever to be offered in any sporting event up to that time.

After five games, the Browns were leading the Sox three games to two. A fourth win would signal a complete victory. The sixth game was being played in St. Louis that October afternoon. It looked as if the series would go the entire seven games. The Stockings were leading three to one in the eighth inning. On the mound for Chicago was John Clarkson, famous for his exquisite control, and one of the best known ballplayers in the world. Catching was Mike "King" Kelly. Cap Anson was in his customary spot on first base, and out in center field was Billy Sunday.

Clarkson got ahead of the first batter, Curt Welch, the Browns' center fielder. But then Welch bunted one of Clarkson's fast balls and never even stopped at first when the hurry-up throw to Cap Anson went wild. The St. Louis crowd jumped to their feet, sensing that a rally had begun. But when the next two batters popped out they again resigned themselves to yet another game before victory.

Bushong was the next batter. Clarkson, with victory close at hand, tried too hard and walked him. Up came little Arlie Latham with the tying run at first base. He was the Browns' third baseman, and it was said that he never grew an inch until he was eighteen, and very little after that. St. Louis fans began to cheer again, and then Mike Kelly let out a bellow from behind the plate.

"He's got a flat bat!" Kelly shouted. "He can't use that bat."

The umpire checked and sure enough, Arlie had whittled one side of his bat so he could place a bunt with less danger of fouling. As the ump sent him back for another bat the crowd jeered at the umpire. "Ten men! Ten men!" they screamed.

New bat in hand, Arlie took his stance again. As he did he caught the characteristic jerk of Mike Kelly's head that meant an inside pitch. The ball came in fast and Arlie placed it right between Sunday and the left fielder Dalrymple. Both men took after it and Arlie headed toward first. Curt Welch scored; Bushong scored. Arlie pulled up at third and the score was tied.

The three-to-three tie continued into the tenth inning with neither team able to get ahead. Billy was playing deep center in deference to Curt Welch's batting ability, but Curt knocked one right over second for a pretty stand-up single. Two batters later, he was standing on third with only ninety feet between him and the world championship.

Doc Bushong, the St. Louis catcher, was up next. Clarkson knew he had to keep it high in order to avoid giving Bushong anything he could hit on the ground. Just as he started to wind up, he saw Welch scurry away from third and head for home plate. In order to give Kelly a chance to trap the runner, Clarkson sent the ball down inside and high. But it was too high. As Mike Kelly grabbed for the ball it bounced off his fingers and toward the fence. Welch hit the dirt hard and slid across the plate with the winning run. Kelly shook both his fists at the sky and flung his glove and mask clear over the grandstand. The St. Louis Browns were the champions of the world. Billy's White Stockings had won six National League pennants during the previous ten years, but the world championship was not yet theirs.

6

The Game of Life

"Hey, Billy, you gonna spend all day in bed? Let's go have some fun." Mike Kelly pounded on the door and continued to shout until Sunday finally poked his head out. It was Sunday afternoon and no game was scheduled. Most of the ballplayers had taken the opportunity to catch up on some extra rest. But now they were ready to hit the town.

"Come on, Billy," Clarkson called to the center fielder. "Let's go get bowled."

Billy had always done some drinking with his teammates, though he seldom got drunk. His future was too great a worry to him, not to mention that Cap Anson wouldn't allow ballplaying after drinking.

"Look at the fellows who used to be the greats," Billy often said to Gore and Dalrymple. "Where are they now? Living off booze, and panhandling. Is that where I'm headed?"

But the others reassured him "You know how to handle booze and money." So off they would go for another weekend on the city of Chicago.

This Sunday was no exception. By late afternoon they had visited most of the saloons on State Street, and there were a lot of saloons to visit. The players were so tanked up when they came out of the last saloon that Kelly, who was already being supported by Clarkson, dropped to the curb.

"Sorry, fellows," he slurred. "Can't go any further. Just leave me here, and I'll find my own way back later."

"Wouldn't leave you behind," Clarkson growled, and dropped down next to him, followed by all the other players. It was then they noticed the portable pump organ and the singing on the other side of State Street.

"It's a band, fellows," mumbled Dalrymple, "and singers. Let's listen. I like singing."

It was a band, but not a band with a lot of instruments. It was a mission band from the Pacific Garden Mission just down State Street a few blocks. It was a street meeting and the entire White Stockings team listened.

The songs were new to most of the fellows, but for Billy they brought back memories of the days when his mother took him and his brothers to the little Methodist church near their home in Iowa. The testimonies sparked no response in the rest of the men, but for Billy the words of faith and love for Jesus Christ stirred in his heart a recollection of his mother's prayers.

Then the testimonies were over and the mission workers were singing a final song.

> Where is my wandering boy tonight,
> The boy of my favorite dreams. . .

"That's a song my mother used to sing, fellows." Billy started to stagger to his feet, but Gore, who was next to him on the curb, pulled him back down again.

"That's all right, Bill. We like our mothers, too. But we're big boys now."

Billy sat back down while the group across the street began to pack up their instruments. But one of the men from the mission had noticed the group on the curb and crossed the street to talk to them.

"Say, fellows, how about coming down to the Pacific Garden Mission for our service this evening? I'm sure you'll enjoy it. You can hear drunkards tell how they have been saved from booze, and girls tell how they have been saved from the red-light district."

Again Billy tried to get up, and again his teammate pulled him down.

"The night's still young," sang out Kelly, who had to be supported even to sit up straight.

"Religion and baseball don't mix," added Clarkson, who was holding Kelly up.

But Dalrymple reached over and knocked Gore's hand loose from Billy's arm. "Let him go, fellows, if that's what he wants. Who knows but what it's what all of us need."

Loosed from his teammate's grip, Billy hoisted himself to his feet. "I'd like to go to your Pacific Garden Mission," he told the worker. And then he turned back to the men. "Fellows, I'm through. I am going to Jesus Christ. We have come to a parting of the ways."

Billy found himself really enjoying the singing and the testimonies at the mission that night. But he was particulary impressed by Colonel and Mrs. Clark, the founders of the mission. He began to attend services at the mission regularly to watch how, night after night, with a consecration that never tired, they labored to bring spiritual and physical help to the motley crowd of men and women who floated past on the streets. For most of the people at the mission,

Pacific Garden was the last stop this side of destruction. But the Clarks, through their love, were able to make this for many of the drifters the first stop on the way to a completely new life. It was these testimonies of transformation that quickened an interest in the ballplayer.

"I've cut down on my drinking," Billy told Mrs. Clark one evening after the service was over.

"That's good, Billy," the saintly woman responded. "But it's not enough. There will be people in hell who've never touched a drop of whisky."

"I've become so honest with my money that Cap Anson has put me in charge of the gate receipts," the ballplayer went on.

"That's commendable, too," she answered. "But just being honest won't get you to Heaven. You need to come to the foot of the cross, gaze up at the crucified Savior, and place all of your sin upon Him."

Conversations like that bothered Billy, but still he did not give in. One of his biggest worries was the team. No professional ballplayers in those days had anything to do with religion or church. The other members of his team razzed him for attending the mission meetings. He could imagine what they would say if he accepted Christ. Baseball was for men. Church was for women and children. So Billy went to the mission, and listened, and waited.

But one night he could wait no longer. As Colonel Clark gave the invitation to accept Christ Billy rose from where he was sitting and in his own words, he "staggered out of sin and into the arms of the Savior."

Before he got back to the boarding house where he stayed, the word of his conversion had already preceded him. One of the other boarders had been at the mission that night, and had taken it upon himself to inform Billy's teammates that their right fielder had 'gotten religion.'

That night Billy could not sleep for thinking about the team and fearing the horselaughs he would get the next morning for taking his stand with Jesus Christ. The team always met at the ballpark at ten o'clock. Everyone else was there when Billy arrived. The first man to meet him was Mike Kelly. Billy braced himself for the laughter, but instead Mike stuck out his hand.

"Bill, I'm proud of you. Religion's not my long suit, but I'll help you all I can."

Up came Anson, Clarkson, Dalrymple, and the rest of the team, every one of them with words of encouragement.

And then came Gore. He was the one Billy feared the most, the one who had tried to hold him back that Sunday afternoon on State Street. Gore didn't say a word. But he offered Billy his hand and a tear glistened in the corner of his eye. Billy knew then they were all on his side.

They were playing Detroit that afternoon. The two teams were neck and neck for the league championship. Clarkson was pitching and Sunday was out in right field. John Clarkson was in rare form. The White Stockings were leading in the ninth with two men already out. But there were also men on second and third ready to tie the score.

Clarkson's pitching style was unique. He had a hole dug in the mound for his foot, and when he stuck his foot into that hole his hand would come around and all the way down to the ground. Somehow the ball would go down and then dance back up again just before it got to the batter.

"You know what to do," Billy yelled from right field. "Keep them up now, and we've got 'em."

Clarkson wound up and bent down, as always. But

when he released the ball, his right foot slipped and
the ball went in fast and low.

Charlie Bennett, the Detroit catcher and one of their
best batters, was waiting. He swung hard, and the
crack when bat met ball could be heard across the
entire field.

Billy had turned and headed for the right field fence
as soon as he saw that the ball was going in low. From
over his shoulder he watched the ball rise. He knew
it was far over his head, but still he ran.

The bleachers, filled beyond capacity, had spilled
many of their spectators into the field, and as he ran,
Billy shouted, "Stand back!"

With an eye still on the ball, and the crowd parting
before him like the Red Sea before Moses, Billy was
sure that the ball was going over the fence. So he
prayed. It was not a very theological prayer, just
something like, "God, if You ever helped a mortal

man, help me now to get that ball, and You don't have much time."

Jumping over a bench someone had hauled onto the field, Billy stopped where he thought the ball would come down. But he had guessed short. It was still going over his head. He jumped as high as he could, shoved his left hand out as far as it would go, and felt the thud as the ball hit his glove. The momentum carried him to the ground under a team of horses waiting for their driver, but somehow he held onto the ball.

Tom Johnson, Cleveland, Ohio, at the time, was the first to reach the jubilant Billy.

"Here's a ten, Bill," he cried, stuffing the money into Billy's pocket. "Buy yourself the best hat in Chicago."

Then the other players were on him, pummeling him and cheering him all the way into the clubroom. Finally it quieted down enough for him to get in a word.

"Thanks, fellows. But it wasn't just me out there this afternoon. It wasn't just Billy who caught that ball. It was Billy and God."

And all the men knew that that's the way it would be from then on. Billy and God.

7

Courting
Nell Thompson

Billy Sunday had been a Christian for only a short while when someone from the Young Men's Christian Association heard about the White Stockings player who had accepted Christ, and invited him to one of their meetings.

"Say, Billy," he was asked one night. "Have you ever considered doing some speaking about Christ?"

"You mean public speaking? Getting up in front of a crowd of people? That's not for me."

"Why not?" his friend persisted. "You're up in front of people all the time at the ball field. Many more people than you'd ever face in the average church."

"That's different."

"What do you mean, that's different? People are people, aren't they? Besides, I need to find someone to speak next Sunday night here at the 'Y' and I think you're the one for the job. How about it?"

The more he thought about it, the less objection

he could find for speaking. It had been a long time since his days in elocution class, but he had enjoyed giving speeches and couldn't really think of any good reason why he wouldn't enjoy it as much now.

So the next Sunday night the talk at the Y.M.C.A. was on "Earnestness in the Christian Life," and the speaker was Chicago White Stockings ballplayer, Billy Sunday.

Soon other opportunities opened up and Billy found that many of his Sundays were spent giving his one talk. But he found that memorizing someone else's speech had been one thing, while preparing his own speech was another matter altogether. Convinced by his initial attempts at public speaking that he needed a coach, just as he had needed a batting coach when he first entered the pro leagues, he enrolled at Evanston Academy. Evanston was the preparatory school for Norhtwestern University. His speech teacher and coach was Dean Cumnock.

In return for his studies that winter, Billy coached the college baseball team. The baseball team had one of their best seasons ever, and Billy's diction improved tremendously. He learned to say, "I did it," instead of, "I done it." And he discovered that what he said was every bit as important as how he said it.

When the season ended in 1887, A. G. Spaulding, unhappy with the team effort that year, decided that some changes needed to be made. Mike Kelly was sold to the Boston team for the unheard of amount of $10,000. Several of the others were traded as well, with Billy ending up as a member of the Pittsburgh team.

Normally the change would not have bothered Billy. Playing ball for one team was little different than playing ball for someone else. But in addition to the fact that he now followed Christ, someone else had come

into his life. Her name was Helen Thompson and it
had begun when he first started attending Jefferson
Avenue Presbyterian Church after his conversion.

"Pleased to meet you, Rev. Cuthbertson." Billy,
shaking hands with the minister on his way out of the
service, was ill at ease in the high starched collar and
large tie men were expected to wear to church services. "I enjoyed your service very much."

"It's been good to have you in attendance," the
minister responded. "Tell me, have you had a chance
to meet any of our other young people yet?"

Billy shook his head, hoping to discourage the
minister. He was not at all sure he wanted to meet
anyone when he was wearing a starched collar. His
baseball suit was certainly much more comfortable.

"We have a Christian Endeavor meeting here at
the church each Sunday night," the pastor went on.
"You would be more than welcome to attend."

"Thank you, sir. I will consider it." And with that
the ballplayer turned to go. But the pastor wasn't
finished yet.

"And just so you will know someone when you
come this evening let me take you right over here and
introduce you to these young people." Before Billy
could protest, he found himself following the receding
back of the minister as they crossed the foyer. Billy
noticed with a certain amount of relief that all of the
young men were in high collars and must be at least
as uncomfortable as he was.

"Archie Campbell. Allow me to introduce you to
Billy Sunday."

Billy stuck out his hand, but the expected response
did not come. Instead Archie ignored the outstretched
palm and turned to the girls who were standing next
to him.

"I didn't know ballplayers bothered going to church," he smirked.

Sunday's first reaction was to slug him. Instead he swallowed his pride. "Some ballplayers don't bother about church," he murmured, thinking about his fellow teammates who had at least encouraged him to stand for the Lord instead of making fun like this young man from the church.

Rev. Cuthbertson moved Billy hurriedly on to some of the other youths in an attempt to smooth over the situation.

"Libby Steward. Billy Sunday."

Billy bowed low over Libby's hand and was just coming up when he got a good glimpse of the next person the minister was introducing.

"Helen Thompson. I want you to meet Billy Sunday."

Again Billy bent low over the young lady's hand,

hoping she would not see the telltale red that was
spreading up his neck. She was definitely the most
beautiful girl he had ever seen. She was wearing what
was obviously a tailor-made jacket with tight sleeves
set high on the shoulders, giving what was called a
"kick-up" effect. The bustle on the skirt was very
pronounced and her hat was decorated with birds,
feathers, and ribbons. But it was none of those which
caught his eye as he straightened up from his bow.
Instead it was the laughing gleam in her eye that told
him she was indeed aware of the impression she had
made on him and that she was pleased to have done so.

"I'm very happy to meet you, Miss Thompson,"
he managed.

Billy was soon attending Jefferson Avenue Church
on Wednesdays for prayer meeting as well as on
Sunday morning for the preaching and Sunday evening for Christian Endeavor. He always took a certain seat along the wall where he could keep one eye
on the minister and the other on "Nell" Thompson.
Though he enjoyed the services immensely and was
even considering joining the church, there was one
disappointment week after week. Every time he saw
Nell she was keeping company with none other than
Archie Campbell.

Then one Wednesday Archie was absent from the
service, and Billy grasped his opportunity.

"May I see you home tonight, Miss Thompson?"

To his chagrin, the very prim and proper Helen
Thompson began to laugh.

"See me home? But I only live across the street."

"I know where you live." Billy pressed his case with
the same enthusiasm he put into chasing high fly balls
in center field. "But we could go the other way—
around the block."

Faced with such an offer from one who had

obviously screwed up a great deal of courage even to talk with her, Helen agreed. Almost half an hour later they finally arrived at the gate to her house, directly across the street from the front door of the church.

The next Sunday came, and still no Archie. Billy could tell that Nell was miffed with her beau, and he pressed his own case again. By the time Archie came back to church, Billy and Nell had moved their talks from the front gate into the Thompsons' parlor and onto a sofa just large enough for the two of them.

As Billy's interest in Helen Thompson began to grow, he realized that there were many problems involved. Her father was a well-to-do dairyman and ice cream manufacturer who did not entirely approve of his daughter's being courted by a professional baseball player. Even though he allowed her little brother, William, Jr., to serve as bat boy for the White Stockings, the idea of Helen and a ballplayer spending so much time together did not sit well.

Billy's other problem was one that had nothing to do with Helen's family. But he knew he had to tell her about it. One night he got the courage to do so. They were seated on that sofa in the parlor when he brought up the subject.

"Nell, there's something I really ought to tell you."

"What's that, Bill?"

"You won't get mad, will you?"

Nell shrugged her shoulders and laughed. "That depends on what you tell me. Give me a try."

"Well, I worked for several summers on the Northwestern Line out of Burlington, Iowa. The engineer in the cab next to mine had a daughter by the name of Clara, and, well . . . we went together for three years."

"And I was dating Archie Campbell when you met me. That didn't stop you, did it?"

Billy half grinned, remembering how much he had
hated seeing her with Archie. But still it wasn't
finished. "Nell, it was more than just seeing her. We
were engaged to be married and—"

"Well, you didn't marry her, did you?" Nell
interrupted.

"No, and I can't now because she's not a Christian, and the Bible says that a believer should never
marry in an unequal yoke."

"Well then," Nell folded her hands on her lap and
spoke as if the whole matter was settled. "There's only
one thing you can do. Go back to Iowa and get things
straightened out with Clara before our relationship
goes one step further."

"But, Nellie," Bill protested. "It's all over between
us. I just thought I should tell you."

"You may think it is. But she probably doesn't.
No, that's the right thing to do, and I won't see you
again until you have done it."

That didn't leave him with much choice at all, so
the next weekend Billy made a trip back to Iowa to
see Clara. When he returned to Chicago, the first
place he visited was the Thompson home. Nell met
him at the door.

"Well, what happened?" she asked. "Did she get
mad at you?"

Billy stared at his shoes and shook his head no.

"Did she cry?"

Again Billy shook his head, and then blurted out
his awful confession. "I didn't have the nerve to tell
her, Nell. I've decided to write her a letter."

That didn't sit very well with Nell. But even his
short absence during the trip back to Iowa had convinced her of how much she cared about him, and
she kept seeing him anyway.

The evening of New Year's Eve they went to a

watchnight service at the church and then returned
to the Thompsons' residence to see in the New Year.
Nell was beautiful that night. She was wearing an ox-
blood cashmere dress with a lynx neckpiece thrown
around her shoulders. Her parents had given her the
fur for Christmas.

Even little William seemed to sense that something
special was up that night, and the entire family left
the courting couple alone in the parlor. Just before
the church bells ushered in the new year of 1888, Billy
screwed up his courage.

"Nell," he pleaded. "Will you marry me? Now?"

Nell smiled until he thought she was going to laugh
at him as she had the first time he asked to take her
home. But she didn't laugh. "Yes, Bill. I've been
waiting for you to ask."

Since Sunday had been traded to Pittsburgh they
had to wait until near the end of the next baseball
season so he could save enough money to support her.

Nell and Billy were certain they could live on love,
but Mr. Thompson wanted to be sure his daughter
would be well cared for. So they set the date for
September 5, 1888.

That gave Billy toward the end of the baseball
season to save his earnings and find them a place to
live in Pittsburgh. And it gave Nell and her mother
time to plan the most beautiful wedding Jefferson
Avenue Church had ever seen.

Billy had realized from the time he first met Helen
Thompson that she was an organizer. And he knew
that was exactly what he needed. Ever since he had
missed all those meals as a young boy in the orphanage
he had needed someone to watch the clock for him.
Nell's Scottish heritage and his implicit trust in her
judgment qualified her to become from the very start,
Billy's business manager.

And so the ceremony at the church went like clockwork.

But Billy, not Nell, had planned the honeymoon. First they went over to the ballpark because Billy's old team the White Stockings were in town for a home game. By special invitation they sat with Mr. Spaulding himself in his reserved box seats.

After the game Helen's parents drove them to the train depot in their landau, a horse-drawn carriage with hickory running gear, wrought iron brackets, and the new solid rubber tires which had just come into use. There the newlyweds climbed on the train and headed off to their new home in Pittsburgh, Pennsylvania.

Billy had been with the Pittsburgh Pirates for only one season after being traded by the White Stockings. The team was having a fairly good season, but Billy was staying as busy off the field as he was on it. He had been invited to teach a boys' Sunday school class in one of the churches in the area. And churches in many of the towns where the team traveled to play would invite him to give his testimony. After one such meeting in a Chicago church the papers reported:

> Center fielder Billy Sunday made a three-base hit at Farwell Hall last night. There is no other way to express the success of his first appearance as a speaker in Chicago. His audience was made up of about five hundred men, who didn't know much about his talents as a preacher, but could all remember his galloping to second base with his cap in his hand.

Nell was proud of her new husband, proud of his ballplaying, and proud of his speaking out for Christ. And Billy wanted his new bride to be proud of him. He had always put his total effort into everything he did, and that was to be the case in his marriage as well as in baseball and his new life for Christ.

The first game back with the team after his wedding, Billy knew that new Mrs. Sunday was up in the
stands watching. And so did everyone else in the
stands by the time the game was over. Billy caught
every ball that came anywhere near him, hit two home
runs with men on base, and they won the game hands
down.

8

Signing with God's Team

"All right, guys. It's time to get started with our Sunday school lesson." Billy Sunday, still somewhat uncomfortable in a starched collar, tried to get the attention of the ten boys sitting in front of him. The lesson they were supposed to be studying was the "Woman at the Well," but the boys were far more interested in the man at the bat.

"Did you really round the bases in fourteen seconds flat while you were with the White Stockings, Mr. Sunday?"

"My dad and I came to see you play yesterday. Do you think the Pittsburgh team will win the championship this year?"

"Tell us about the time—"

"Wait just a minute. If you want to talk about baseball you'll have to wait until tomorrow." Billy opened his Bible once again to the lesson for the day. "This is the Lord's day, and we're going to study His Book."

Reluctantly the boys turned their attention from baseball to the Bible. But they listened more closely than they had to their previous teacher, happy that Billy Sunday himself was their teacher.

Billy was often asked to teach Sunday school in the different cities where his team played during the week. His testimony for Christ was becoming almost as well known as his reputation as a baseball player. But he always tried to focus interest on Christ rather than on himself. In fact, he refused to speak anywhere unless they would allow him to give a public invitation for people to accept Christ as Savior. "Why should I waste my time to go there if I can't bring people to Christ?" he would say to Nellie.

Feeling the importance of Bible training for himself since he was being called on to teach others, Billy spent his winters at the Y.M.C.A. in Chicago, studying the Bible and doing what he could to help around the place.

One evening as he stood on the street giving out tickets and inviting men to a dinner and meeting which was going to be held at the Y's Farwell Hall, a young man approached him.

"Hey, Pard. Will you give me a dime?"

"No, sir." Billy shook his head firmly, knowing the man would only spend it on more drinks, of which he had already had enough, from the looks of it.

"I want to get something to eat."

"My time is up at ten o'clock. Wait until then and I'll buy you something to eat. But I won't give you any money."

"Thank you. I'll stay."

Billy took the man with him into the hall for the service and then, true to his promise, took him out for a hot meal. As they ate, Billy began to share with him the story of the love of Christ. To his surprise the young man, whose name was Charles, began to cry.

"Don't talk to me about love. Listen to my story and then you'll know why."

Charles leaned across the table toward Billy and began to tell his story.

"There were three boys in my family. When my father died his will said that the money was to be divided between us, with nothing for Mother. I guess he thought he would outlive her. Anyway, I took my money and left home, drinking and gambling as I went. Finally I reached Denver and got a position as railroad man. Mother kept writing to me, but I never read the letters, just threw them into the firebox. But one day, I decided to read one.

"It said,' Dear Son, I haven't heard from you directly, but I am sure that you must need a mother's love in the far-off West. Unless you answer this in a reasonable time I'm coming to Denver to see you. Your loving mother.'

"I threw the letter in the fire and paid no more heed to it. But one day about two weeks later I saw a woman coming down the track and said to the engineer, 'That looks like my mother.' Then do you know what I did?"

"Why, you climbed down out of that engine, kissed her, and asked God to forgive you," Billy responded.

"I did nothing of the kind. I was so low-down I wouldn't even talk to her. She followed me up and down the switchyard and even over to my boarding-house, but I just pushed her aside and set off for the saloon. For four days she tried to talk to me and finally she left. That's nine years ago, Mr. Sunday, and I have never seen nor heard from her since. And then you talk to me about love. No one could ever love me again."

"But someone does," Billy told Charles. And there in the restaurant Billy told Charles about Jesus, the one whose love had captured Billy's heart already. Then Charles bowed his head and asked Jesus to be his Savior.

Experiences such as that, plus his study of the Bible at the Y.M.C.A., soon convinced Billy that he was wasting his time in professional baseball. Leading men like Charles to Christ was more exciting than hitting a bases-loaded home run. But he had signed a contract for another three years with the Philadelphia team, which had traded him with Pittsburgh in 1891. He saw no way of getting out of it. He even went so far as to send a telegram to Philadelphia asking to be released. But the answer came back, "No. Why should we release you? People like to see you play. We've signed you up for three years."

"There's only one way, Billy," said Nell. "If the Lord wants you to quit baseball, He can get you out of that contract. We'll just have to pray about it."

So Billy started to pray. To Billy that just meant talking to God, and so he talked. "Lord, I've been trying to do some work for you down here with the Y.M.C.A. And Lord, it's been a lot of fun. I think maybe you want me to do it all the time, but there's the matter of this contract. Now, Lord, if I don't get my release from the club by March 25 when we're supposed to report for the new season, then I'll just figure You still want me to play baseball. All right, Lord?"

On March 17, St. Patrick's Day, he was leading a noon meeting at Farwell Hall when a friend brought in the letter he was waiting for. It was from Colonel Rogers, the owner of his club, releasing him from his contract.

Jim Hart, of the Cincinnati team, had already heard

about it and came right up on the platform where Billy was sitting.

"Bill, I have a check here for $500. Sign up with us and you'll get one like it every month." Five thousand dollars for one season, Bill"

"No." Billy shook his head. "I promised God that if He gave me my release before March 25 I would quit baseball."

"You're a fool," Jim told him. "Why, you're just now beginning to earn real money in baseball. What about your family? How are you going to support them?" The country is in a slump! People don't even have enough food to eat, and you're turning down a five thousand dollar contract?"

But Billy would not listen. He had made a promise and that was that. Friends appealed to Nell to talk some sense into him. But she just smiled and said, "He promised God to quit. There's nothing to reconsider."

Sunday went to work for the Chicago Y.M.C.A. at a salary of $83.33 per month. That was barely enough money to pay the house rent, and then a baby daughter came along and there was a third mouth to feed. But Billy was happy. He walked to work to save cabbie fare. Helen made his old clothes over and dyed them to look like new. They both were agreed not to appeal to her parents for help, but even Mr. Thompson approved of Billy's new devotion to Christ and found ways to help the struggling family from time to time.

The new job not only involved small pay but long hours. Often Billy put in fourteen hours a day. He preached regularly on the street corners of Chicago, found speakers for meetings at Farwell Hall, handed out religious literature in saloons, and conducted prayer meetings. There were times when he grew

discouraged and considered going back into baseball.

One time after a particularly hard week, he arrived home late Friday night with big news. J. Palmer O'Neill of the Pittsburgh Pirates had contacted him and invited him to rejoin the team.

"They need an outfielder bad," he told Nell, "and they're willing to pay two thousand a month."

Nell thought how much their little daughter Helen needed new clothes and how long it had been since she had been able to buy a new outfit, but she shook her head. "You play for the Pirates if you want to, but I thought all along that a life of Christian service was what you wanted. No man can serve two masters."

Billy grinned somewhat sadly and pulled her and little Helen close, "Thank you, Nell. I'm glad someone in this house has backbone."

When Billy got the most discouraged, he would think about the men who had played ball with him and what had happened to them. In fact, he sometimes ran into them even in his new job.

Frank Flint, who had been the pitcher on the Chicago team, now spent many a night on a table in a stale-beer joint. Often Billy would see him and talk to him about Christ. But Flint drank incessantly and was usually in too much of a stupor to understand and respond.

One winter day Flint staggered out of a beer joint when a fit of coughing seized him. A woman coming down the street recognized him and called a carriage to take him to the hospital. As the hospital staff leaned over Frank, trying to nurse him back to health, he whispered, "Send for Billy."

When Billy came into the room, he could hardly recognize Frank Flint as the same man who had once terrorized the batters on the professional circuit. He took the man's hand and gripped it hard.

"Bill," Frank gasped, "I can still hear the bleachers cheer when I made a hit that won the game. But it don't do me any good now. Billy, if I don't reach home and the Supreme Umpire calls me out, won't you say a few words over me?"

"Of course I will," Sunday promised, "but it's not too late for you, Frank. You can still come to Christ."

Even as Billy talked, he saw Frank struggling as he had years ago on the diamond trying to reach home plate. He rounded third, going hard trying to beat the throw. But the Umpire of the Universe shouted, "You're out!" and the great gladiator of the ball diamond was no more.

It was times like that, at the bedside of Frank Flint, that convinced Billy he had indeed made the right

choice. He had signed on with God's team and the
benefits were eternal.

After three years with the Y.M.C.A., Billy had met
many men who were serving God in various capacities
around the country. Some of them began to notice
him and to realize that God might perhaps have even
greater things in store for the former ballplayer. One
of these was P. P. Bilhorn, the song writer. Bilhorn
worked with J. Wilbur Chapman on occasion as his
song leader, and he knew that Chapman was looking
for an "advance man" for his evangelistic meetings.

"You really ought to take a look at this Sunday
fellow," he told Chapman on one of those occasions
when they met. "I've never seen a fellow with more
enthusiasm and vitality. Why, he serves the Lord just
like he used to play ball, with everything he's got."

So the next time Evangelist Chapman was in
Chicago, he took a good look at Billy and liked what
he saw.

"I need someone like you, Sunday. Someone who
can go to each town before I get there and rent a hall
and raise enough money to pay for it. I don't like having to take offerings for expenses after I get to town.
How about it?"

Dr. Chapman did not have to ask twice. As much
as he enjoyed his work in Chicago, Billy saw this as
an opportunity to reach even more men and women
with the gospel. Dr. Chapman was one of the best
known evangelists in the nation at that time, along
with D. L. Moody and R. A. Torrey. Working with
him would be an education Billy could not afford to
miss. Besides, the forty dollars a week the evangelist
offered him would be a tremendous blessing now that
two boys had joined the little girl in the Sunday
household.

For two and a half years Billy traveled as "advance

man'' for Dr. Chapman. He went into a town, organized committees to oversee the meeting, and rented a hall. If a hall could not be found, he set up a tent. When Chapman arrived Billy led singing, although Billy admitted himself that he had nothing to offer to the song service except ''vim, vigor, and tabasco sauce.'' And after each service he counseled with those who had come forward to learn more about Christ. Then he would get the hall back in shape for the meeting the next night.

Before a month had gone by, Dr. Chapman knew he had found the ideal advance man in Billy Sunday. He had a contagious enthusiasm that inspired revival crowds and prepared them for the preaching. He was persuasive, able to get people to do almost anything he asked. During one meeting on the east coast, President Benjamin Harrison was recognized coming in the door.

''Why, Mr. President,'' Billy called from the platform, ''how good of you to come. We've been saving a seat for you right up here on the platform.'' Billy turned and pointed to the only empty seat left on the stage, the one he had just risen from. ''You will come up here and join us, won't you, Mr. President?''

To Dr. Chapman's amazement and to the amazement of the other men on the platform, the president smiled and accepted the invitation. The only person not surprised was Billy Sunday.

One night as Billy was introducing the service, anticipating the arrival of Dr. Chapman on a passenger train, the Vandalia, an urgent message was handed to him by one of the ushers.

''A wreck on the Vandalia has delayed my arrival,'' read the telegram. ''Please take the service entirely. J. Wilbur Chapman.''

Without losing a beat of the song service, Billy

moved through the planned program to the time of
the message. Then he began to preach, quoting almost
word for word one of Dr. Chapman's messages. He
had heard them all so many times that he was able
to preach them as if they were his own.

The newspapers picked up on that meeting immediately and reported that Billy Sunday had "proved
he was just as capable with the Bible as he was with
a bat."

When Christmas, 1895, arrived, the evangelistic
team was given a few weeks off. Billy hurried back
to Chicago to spend time with Nellie and his three
children. It was the perfect holiday. Plenty of snow,
lots of gifts, and lots of love.

At the height of the holiday festivities a knock came
on the door of the Sunday home.

"I'll get it," Billy called over his shoulder to the
family.

"Telegram for Mr. Billy Sunday," said the
uniformed man at the door.

"I'm Billy Sunday. Thank you." Billy shut the
door and turned back into the house.

"Who's it from, Billy?" asked Nell.

Sunday tore open the telegram and read the
message aloud.

"Have decided to quit evangelistic work. John
Wanamaker has asked me to take the pastorate of a
church in Philadelphia. Have cancelled all future
meetings. Thank you for your good work. Merry
Christmas. J. Wilbur Chapman."

Billy couldn't believe his own eyes. "I never
dreamed he would leave the evangelistic field and go
back to a church," he told Nellie.

Christmas! And no prospects for a job of any kind.
Suddenly the holiday that had been so promising had
turned black.

9

The Sawdust Trail Begins

What had started out to be a wonderful holiday season turned to one of gloom after Billy received Dr. Chapman's telegram. Although he had been away from it for almost six years, Billy began to think seriously about going back into baseball. He had given up baseball for the job with the Y.M.C.A., and had given up that job to work with the Chapman evangelistic team. Now with a wife and three small children to support, he was without any job.

It was during those weeks that he began to realize the spiritual strength of the woman he had married. Every time he became discouraged, she reassured him that he had not made a mistake in quitting baseball or in leaving the Y.M.C.A.

"You've learned so much from Dr. Chapman," Nellie reminded him.

"Sure. I've learned how to set up a tent and how to take an offering, and even a little bit about preaching. But how can I use any of those things here in Chicago? Go to work for a circus or something?''

"Now, Billy. Romans 8:28 is still in your Bible, isn't it?''

"Of course it is. But I fail to see how anything good could come out of losing my job. Why, Dr. Chapman had meetings booked all the way through next summer. And more churches were writing him all the time.''

"Well, why don't you ask him to let you take some of those meetings? The churches will have to get someone.''

"I couldn't do that. Dr. Chapman was well known. Some of those are the biggest churches in the country. They would never allow a former ballplayer to preach in their pulpits. No, I'll just have to write to Jim Hart up in Cincinnati, or maybe go over and talk to Mr. Spaulding.''

"You'll do nothing of the kind, Mr. Sunday.''

"But, Ma, I have to feed you and the children.''

"Don't you worry about us. You promised God you would work for Him, and there's no discharge in His war.''

"But He does pay His soldiers, doesn't He? What's going to happen?''

Mrs. Sunday just smiled. "Romans 8:28,'' she said again. "It's still in the Book.''

Billy knew she was right. There was no way he could go back into professional baseball, but at the same time there had to be something he could do with all that he had learned at the Y.M.C.A. and with Dr. Chapman. So he waited. And he prayed. It wasn't easy to pray because he knew he was a little angry with God for giving Dr. Chapman a church and not thinking about him. But still he prayed.

Then one day he was looking through the mail and

came across a letter from a place in Iowa called
Garner.

"Who do we know in Garner, Iowa, who would
be sending us a late Christmas card," he called over
his shoulder to Nellie, who was preparing a meal in
the kitchen.

"I don't know. Better open it and see."

Puzzled by the strange postmark, Sunday tore open
the letter and read it, first to himself and then aloud
to Nellie, who had come to stand in the doorway.

> Dear Rev. Sunday,
> You do not know me. But I am the pastor of the
> Presbyterian Church here in Garner, Iowa. The Bap-
> tist and Methodist ministers have gone in with me,
> and we are going to hold a city-wide revival. We have
> already rented the opera house here in Garner. We
> would like to know if you would be our evangelist.
> Please let us know at once if you can come.

Billy looked up to see the gleam in Nellie's eyes.
"I know what you are going to say. Roman 8:28 is
still in the Book."

He sent off a wire that same afternoon, and two
weeks later he was in Garner, Iowa, for eight days
of meetings. The town of Garner had only one thousand population. Though the three Protestant churches in town were uniting in the revival effort, their
total membership came to less than three hundred.
There was no gospel singer, and Billy hadn't had time
to send an advance man to town. So he had to lead
his own choir, raise the expenses, try to get committees organized after the meetings began, and do all
the preaching as well.

Attendance at the meetings started slowly, but soon
the word got around town that the former Chicago
White Stockings outfielder from Marshalltown, Iowa,

was preaching at the opera house. People began to come. Billy gave his old Y.M.C.A. challenge on "Earnestness in the Christian Life" and saw many of the members of the three sponsoring churches come to the altar to rededicate themselves to Christ. They in turn began to bring their friends and neighbors, and attendance grew even more.

After his Y.M.C.A. talk, Billy preached Dr. Chapman's sermons, not having had time to prepare his own. They did not come out the way Dr. Chapman used to preach them, but God blessed the services anyway. People began to walk down the aisle, coming for salvation.

At the end of the week, the Presbyterian pastor who had written to Sunday came to him in great excitement, followed closely by his fellow pastors.

"Rev. Sunday, do you realized what has happened?"

"I think I do. We have seen a great blessing from God this week?"

"Great? It has been tremendous! Garner has never seen anything like it. Do you realize that two hundred and sixty-eight people have walked the aisle to publicly confess their belief in Jesus Christ as personal Savior?"

"You just have to stay another week," one of the other pastors interrupted. "Why, this entire town could come to Christ."

Billy had been smiling broadly as the man talked, but now the smile faded. "I'm sorry, fellows. I would like to stay, really I would. But I just can't."

"But why not? This is revival. Garner will never be the same again."

"I know. And I'm excited, too. But you see, I've had a call from Pawnee City, Nebraska. They want me to come there for a meeting as soon as possible."

"You can go to Pawnee City. But you need to stay here for at least another week first. Things are just getting started."

"Is it the offering?" the Baptist minister interjected. "We would like to have given you more than $68.00. But with the expenses for the opera house and all, it just hasn't been possible. Surely more will come in this next week."

"No, it's not the offering." Billy shook his head. "And the fellowship has been great. Here's the real reason. By tonight I will have preached fourteen sermons. After that, I just don't have any more sermons to preach. I'll have to go on to Pawnee City and start over again on sermons. By tonight I'll be all run out."

So the pastors let him go on to Pawnee City, Nebraska.

During the next five years Billy Sunday held sixty revival meetings in the corn belt of Iowa, Minnesota,

Illinois, Nebraska, and Missouri. The average meeting lasted one week and was held either in the largest cooperating church or in a large hall in town.

Around the turn of the century, Billy began to get some requests from larger towns for a month-long meeting. That in turn meant larger crowds, so he bought a circus tent and set that up in an empty lot to hold the crowds. He often reminded Nell, who had left the children in Chicago with her parents so she could travel with him, about the days when he had suggested that he might get a job setting up circus tents.

As the meetings grew so did Sunday's organization. Fred Fischer joined him in 1900 as his full-time songleader. Fred began to take care of many of the functions Billy himself had done when he was working with Dr. Chapman. Sometimes they even rented a twelve-piece orchestra to accompany the singing. But the biggest help was Mrs. Sunday. She handled the finances of the campaigns, took care of the correspondence and arrangements for the coming meetings, and saw to it that her husband got the proper food and rest.

Then in 1905 an accident occurred which would change forever the character of the Sunday campaigns. A late spring snowstorm dumped ten inches of snow on a tent set up for a meeting in Salida, Colorado. The tent collapsed. Luckily it was during the night so no one was injured. Other quarters had to be found before the revival services could go on. Billy vowed that he would never again use a tent in his campaigns. And out of that vow came his most famous trademark, the ''Billy Sunday Tabernacles.''

10

Billy Sunday Tabernacles

"You could run a locomotive over it and never faze it," Billy Sunday proclaimed loudly to the group of businessmen who were in Perry, Iowa, being shown through the first Billy Sunday Tabernacle ever built. "This platform is so strong that it can even withstand the shock of my type of preaching."

And just to prove his point, the evangelist raced to the platform and leaped about in the style for which he was so famous. He pounded the pulpit, then vaulted over it. "Take that, you old devil!" he shouted, as both feet landed with a thud on the wooden floor. "We've got you on the run now."

The reason Billy was showing the tabernacle to the businessmen of Perry, Iowa, was that they had put up the seven hundred dollars to build it. Ever since the snow had collapsed his revival tent in Salida, Colorado, Bill had been determined never to have a meeting in a tent again. Something more substantial was necessary, but most of the towns had no building large enough to house the crowds that came to hear him preach. To solve the problem, Billy hit upon a completely new idea in American evangelism—he would build his own tabernacle.

Each tabernacle was made almost identical, to previous tabernacles, except for size. They were barn-like structures built out of raw lumber, with no resemblance to a cathedral. The main considerations were sound and safety. The one thousand people who crowded into the Perry tabernacle several times a day could be assured of hearing every whisper of the evangelist. A huge sounding board that looked something like an inverted sugar scoop hung over the platform to bounce the sound of his voice to every corner of the building. The ceiling had been kept low to help the sound carry.

"But the most important factor in the construction of the tabernacle," the evangelist explained to the men, "has been safety. The safety factors include the single-story construction—everyone has his feet on the ground at all times. Every aisle, crosswise and lengthwise, ends in a door. And twenty-five doorkeepers have been specially trained for the campaign.

The concern about safety was a very real one for the Sunday team. Recent events in the nation and around the world had raised people's awareness of safety. Several theaters in the larger cities had been destroyed by fires that were almost impossible to fight. Hundreds of people had lost their lives. The "Boxer" Rebellion in China had been marked by the burning of many churches, including the South Cathedral and the famous Asbury Church. Worst of all, the nation had just endured the assassination of President William McKinley at the Pan-American Exposition

in Buffalo, New York. Some of the businessmen in Perry had received letters threatening to burn down the tabernacle if Billy Sunday actually came to town. And Billy was the last one to think they wouldn't try.

"You can see the fire extinguishers for yourselves. And both firemen and policemen from your fair city have volunteered their time to help us during the meeting."

The organization that was so evident to those Perry businessmen was a characteristic of every Billy Sunday campaign. He had learned from his days in baseball that a batter gets only three strikes and he's out. Billy was determined never to strike out for God.

Each tabernacle constructed in the years following the first one in Perry, Iowa, saw improvement. Behind the platform was added a post office from which the names of the converts in the meetings were sent to the pastors in town every morning.

A nursery for babies was added to one side, far enough away so the service would not be disturbed, but close enough so that the mothers would not worry. One thing Billy could not stand during his preaching was any competition. He would stop right in the middle of a sermon to let a single person walk down the aisle, focusing the attention of everyone in the audience on that person and embarrassing him to the place where no one else was about to try such a thing. If people started to cough, Billy stopped preaching until it was quiet again. He was not about to strike out with anyone just because of someone else's cough. And crying babies? At first he asked the mother to leave, but that was too disruptive. So his doorkeepers were instructed to handle the problem before the service even began. No infant was allowed into the building—all were sent immediately to the nursery.

But one thing that continued to bother Billy for several years was the noise when a crowd of people got to walking on the wooden floors. "Its the limit," he told his assistant, Fred Fischer, many times. They would try to think of a solution, but without success.

Then came a meeting out in lumber country in Oregon. Men from all over the area rallied to put together a Billy Sunday tabernacle. In the course of the construction, the suggestion was made that sawdust be spread in the aisles to keep down the dust, muffle the noise of feet, and even serve as a fire retardant. Immediately Billy knew that he had his answer. To the lumbermen of the northwest, responding to the invitation in the new tabernacle soon became known as "hitting the sawdust trail." Other evangelists, such as Dwight L. Moody and Wilbur J. Chapman, had encouraged converts to "go forward" or "seek the altar." Billy began to challenge them to "hit the sawdust trail." He liked the idea so much that the sawdust became a permanent fixture in his wooden buildings, even after he left the lumber country. And the term "sawdust trail" became a permanent part of people's vocabulary.

The decisions for Christ that were made in the tabernacle were what people noticed as the most obvious result of the Sunday campaigns. But these decisions were really just a small part of the total picture. A Billy Sunday campaign was designed to motivate the cooperating churches to make an impact on their city for Christ. Several months before Billy arrived in a city, an advance man began his work of organizing the churches for revival. Long before a hammer was ever heard in the construction of a tabernacle, people began to meet in the homes of the city to pray for God's blessing on the coming campaign.

The advance man had meetings with an executive committee and divided the city into small sections with a home in each two-block area designated for a cottage prayer meeting. Many times those prayer meetings were held in the homes of the unconverted, and it was normal for many conversions to occur before the evangelist ever reached the city. In Scranton, Pennsylvania, during a three-week period 4,137 prayer meetings were held in private homes with a combined attendance of 68,360 people. The united prayer of so many people was a tremendous factor in the successs of the Sunday campaigns.

While the prayer meetings were being held, the advance man organized other committees as well. An entertainment committee, an ushering committee, a dinner committee, a business women's committee, a building committee, a nursery committee, a personal workers' committee, a decorating committee, a shopmeetings committee, and a choir where all gathered together and instructed as to their duties.

The ushers were drilled in crowd control in addition to their duties of seating the people and taking the offering. Since there were almost always more people trying to get into the meetings than the tabernacle would seat, it took strong men to get the doors shut and hold back the rest of the crowd when the building was full. Oftentimes another five hundred people stood around the outside of the tabernacle listening through the windows after the doors had been closed.

The offering procedure was so smooth that Billy claimed a collection could be received from eight thousand persons in less than three minutes. In a crowd of that size, one hundred ushers were placed at intervals throughout the auditorium. When the song leader announced the offering, they rose quietly but quickly to positions on the aisle at the front of fifty designated sections. At the signal from the song leader they began their practiced collection routine. Half the ushers carried piles of wicker baskets, and marched briskly down the aisles, starting one basket at the end of each bench. The offering baskets passed along the benches to the far end, and the other half of the ushers came along, almost as briskly as the first, and collected all the baskets. At the back of the tabernacle, the baskets were emptied into canvas bank bags. And this all happened before the musicians could complete two stanzas of "Onward Christian Soldiers." The offerings that were collected each night were for the expenses of the meeting. The only offering Mr. Sunday received was a free-will offering taken on the final day of the campaign. From that offering he paid his own expenses and those of his campaign team. Since it was his own income, that was also the way he paid for his home in Winona Lake, Indiana, where Ma Sunday and the children lived while he was out on the campaign trail.

The other big job of the ushers came at the time

of the invitation. The instant Billy Sunday stopped preaching and began to invite penitents to hit the sawdust trail, the ushers were to clear out the front three rows of the tabernacle. Two of the biggest men were to station themselves on either side of the evangelist. As people began to move forward, they took each person's arm, placed his hand in Mr. Sunday's hand, either the right or the left hand depending on which side they were on. Then the next usher took the person by the arm and moved him on to the counselors who had taken their places in the first three rows. No one was allowed to stop and talk to the evangelist, because he was often called upon to shake fifty hands per minute in order to congratulate personally all those who responded to the invitation. All the individual counseling was done by the personal-work secretaries, who talked with each person who responded to the invitation. Then each counselor filled out a decision card, which included name, address, and church preference. It was the decision cards that were sent to the cooperating churches from the tabernacle post office the next morning.

The "sawdust trail" which began in Garner, Iowa, stretched all the way to the West Coast and then back across the country toward the East again. People from the East had heard about Bill Sunday for several years, but even many pastors generally believed that he would do well in the West and Midwest, but "the East would not stand for him." They felt that he was too uncouth, that his messages were too common, and his methods too crude.

Then a group of pastors in the steel and coal town of Pittsburg, Pennsylvania, where Billy had once played baseball, got together to build a tabernacle. There were many predictions of failure, but none of the predictions bothered Billy. He just smiled at Nellie, and together they said, ''Romans 8:28 is still in the Book.''

11

Battling with Booze

"I hate sin. I'll kick it as long as I've got a foot. I'll fight it as long as I've got a fist. I'll butt it as long as I've got a head. I'll bite it as long as I've got a tooth. And when I'm old and fistless, and footless and toothless, I'll gum it, till I go home to glory and it goes home to perdition."

Billy Sunday preached the same way he had played baseball, with everything he had. He raced back and forth across the platform and then, leaping into the air, he doubled up like a jackknife for emphasis. He would bring his fist down so hard on a chair that people feared he had broken his bones. During one of his favorite illustrations about a man who comes home drunk and threatens his wife and daughter, he would catch up a chair on the platform and swing it over his head, then crash the chair against the floor, splintering the legs and casting the wreck from him.

Billy's strongest preaching was reserved for his sermon against drinking. Ever since his days with the Chicago White Stockings, he had seen the effects of alcohol, first on his fellow ballplayers and then on the men who had come to the Y.M.C.A. for spirirual help. Billy had not been preaching long in the Midwest before he gained a reputation as the most effective foe of the liquor business in America.

After his sermon, "Booze, or Get on the Water Wagon," was preached in Fairfield, Iowa, the two freight-wagon express companies in town were faced with a problem. No one would accept the three barrels of beer that had arrived from the brewer. So they sent them back with a note attached, "The cause of refusal is the influence of sermons by Rev. W. Sunday."

In another town the saloon closed for lack of business after one of his revivals. The saloon keeper placed a sign in the window, "Closed by order of Billy Sunday."

In 1908 the Illinois spring elections came in the midst of one of his large campaigns. Since Monday was his day off, Billy usually took a train and traveled to one of the other towns in the state to deliver his "Booze" sermon. When the elections were held, it was found that enough towns had voted "dry" to knock out fifteen hundred saloons.

After a campaign in New Castle, Pennsylvania, it was reported that there were no saloons open in either the city or the county. And though the city had a population of forty thousand, there had been only eighty-three total arrests in the entire two months following the close of the meeting.

But Fairfield, Iowa, and New Castle, Pennsylvania, were not the same as Pittsburgh. Pittsburgh was steel and railroads and liquor. Those men would never listen to an evangelist. And besides that, the brewers and saloon-keepers had vowed to drive him out of town before he even got started. Why, it was rumored that they had raised over ten thousand dollars to fight Billy Sunday.

The tabernacle built for the meeting in Pittsburgh was the biggest one ever yet erected for a Sunday campaign. And that meant some modifications had to be made. The platform was moved more toward the center of the large barn-like structure so people could sit on three sides and be closer to the evangelist. The platform was raised to twenty feet high and a sounding board in the shape of a saucer was hung overhead so all fifteen thousand people could hear Billy's voice. Billy was worried about panic in a crowd that size, so he ordered that the boards on the side of the tabernacle be nailed on with only two nails each. That way, if it became necessary, any section of the wall could quickly be removed to make way for the exit of such a great mass of humanity.

For weeks before the meeting, cottage prayer sessions were held in various homes throughout the city. About a week before Billy arrived, a traveling salesman came into one of the Pittsburgh hotels looking puzzled.

"I just saw the strangest sight I have ever seen in my entire life," he said to the desk clerk.

"And what was that?"

"Women—hundreds of women—parading along the sidewalk. And every last one of them was carrying a Bible."

"What's so strange about that?" the clerk asked, grinning. "They're just going to the ten o'clock Bible study."

"Bible study?" the salesman questioned.

"Certainly. Haven't you heard? Billy Sunday's coming to town."

Had the salesman been back in town the following week, he would have seen an even stranger sight. The

campaign in Pittsburgh began with what was called
a "Sunday-school parade." Promptly at noon on the
day of the first meeting, delegations that had been
gathering most of the morning moved out along a
four-mile prearranged march route. Children too
small to walk were carried in hay wagons, on carts,
and in automobiles. The city even donated two street
sprinkler wagons to carry the children. Several thousand more children and adults marched, all of them
carrying banners and flags, and singing gospel songs.

Twenty thousand people in all marched through the
streets of Pittsburgh, led by Billy and "Ma," along
with the new song leader Homer Rodeheaver. Mr.
Rodeheaver played his trombone and was backed up
by every high school band in town. A platoon of
policeman on horses kept the way clear. Thousands
more people lined the sidewalks. There was no doubt
in anyone's mind that Billy Sunday had arrived.

But still there were those who were sure easterners
would not respond to his preaching. They were just
waiting for his sermon on "Booze" so they could
prove to everyone that steel and coal men were not
about to give up drinking just because of Billy
Sunday's preaching.

They did not have long to wait.

Billy announced his "Booze" sermon after he had
been in Pittsburgh only one week. And he surprised
the crowd by saying, "This will be a service for men
only. No women will be allowed into the tabernacle,
because there would not be room for everyone if we
allowed the women to come."

The skeptics really laughed at that one. Maybe he
could fill the tabernacle with women and Sunday
school kids, but he could never fill it with men.

The night the "Booze" sermon was to be preached,
they had planned to open the doors of the tabernacle

at six o'clock for the seven o'clock meeting. But at five-thirty one of the Pittsburgh policemen sought out the head usher.

"Is there any way we can get you to open the doors early?"

"Don't believe so. What's the problem?"

"Haven't you looked outside?" asked the policeman. "Men are lined up around the entire building and have spilled over into all the streets. Cars are backed up for blocks and it's impossible to get anything moving. Please let some of the men into the building so we can try to get the traffic moving again."

The head usher took one look outside and ordered that the doors be opened. Within fifteen minutes every bench in the place was filled with men, and still there were those outside trying to get in. Large wooden shutters covering screened windows were dropped and the men pushed up close to those, trying to hear and see even a portion of what was going on inside.

Half an hour before the service was scheduled to start, Homer Rodeheaver appeared on the platform with his trombone. He was followed by two pianists and a five-hundred voice choir.

"Guess we might as well get started," he told his pianists. Swinging his trombone to his mouth he began to play, "O, That Will Be Glory for Me." The applause from the men kept all except those in the front rows from even hearing his horn.

For almost an hour Rody kept the men busy. The choir sang, accompanied by the two pianos plus four trumpeters and Mr. Rodeheaver's trombone. The men sang, led by the enthusiastic song leader. For a while Rody simply made weird sounds on his trombone, which made everyone laugh. Then he began giving recognition to delegations. The men from the Bible Brigade had all come dressed in their uniforms, so he had them stand while everyone sang "Onward Christian Soldiers." A group of firemen requested "Let the Lower Lights Be Burning." Homer recognized a delegation from a garment factory and suggested that they sing the Negro spiritual, "I've Got a Robe."

When it came time for the offering, the leader of the railroad delegation came to the platform and announced that his men were giving Billy Sunday an entire hopper car full of coal.

"Since he obviously doesn't need it to heat this place," he joked, "we'll sell it for him and give the money to the campaign."

Then Billy Sunday appeared. Rody was leading a song when the evangelist came onto the platform, but applause began to break out all over the auditorium. The songleader stopped in the middle of the song and joined in the applause as Billy waved and took his seat. As soon as the song was over, it was time for the message that people said gave Satan the shivers.

"Whisky is God's worst enemy and the devil's best friend," Billy declared as he leaned over the pulpit and looked into the eyes of his audience. "The saloon is a liar. There are twelve thousand saloon-keepers in New York City and eight thousand of them have criminal records. I don't think Pittsburgh is too far behind."

He stood at the pulpit for only a minute. His fists were balled up like a fighter entering the ring for hard-hitting, no-holds-barred boxing. Only a minute, and then he flew into action.

"Yes, the saloon is a liar. Every plot that was ever hatched against the government and law was born and bred and crawled out of the grog shop to damn this country." Racing to the edge of the platform he leaned far over the audience, and then he leaned backward in a curve to demonstrate booze crawling out of the grog shop.

"Whisky is all right in its place, but its place is in hell. And I want to see everyone put it there as soon as possible." Racing to the other side of the platform, he again leaned over the edge, so far over that the people below him gasped, afraid he would fall on them. But if Billy Sunday ever fell, it was because he had planned to fall. With perfect athletic control, he jumped and rushed and waved and stamped, first on one side of the platform and then on the other, constantly in motion, emphasizing every word with an appropriate action.

For one hour and forty-five minutes he preached, shedding coat, collar, cuffs, and tie in the process. "The saloon feeds on our boys and destroys the young manhood of our country," he shouted as fifty boys in uniform marched across the stage behind him

waving American flags. "Are you going to let these boys be destroyed or are you going to take your stand for God and country? Can you be counted on to protect your wives and homes, your mothers and the children and the manhood of America?"

With a great leap Billy was on top of the pulpit, arms outstretched, pleading with the vast congregation to take their stand for God. "I've had more sneers and scoffs and insults, and had my life threatened from one end of the land to the other by this God-forsaken gang of thugs and cuttroats, because I have come out uncompromisingly against them. I've taken more dirty, vile insults from this low-down bunch than from anyone on earth, but I've done it for your boys and your wives, and for you. How about it, will you come and take my hand and say, 'Bill, I'll take my stand against booze the very first chance I get.' Come on, let's get every man here on the water wagon."

From every part of the auditorium they started to come. The ushers cleared the people out of the front rows and Billy jumped down from the platform to shake hands. In an unending stream people came. The entire delegation from the Bible Brigade, all of the firemen, and most of the railroad men streamed down the aisle to take their place with Billy in his battle against booze.

From that day on the tabernacle was crowded every time a service was held. Thousands of people "hit the sawdust trail," and even before the meetings were over, invitations had come from Philadelphia and Baltimore and Boston, and even from New York City. Billy Sunday and the sawdust trail were coming to the East. And the booze forces were running scared. People were actually beginning to talk about the possibility of a national law prohibiting the sale and consumption of all alcoholic beverages. But the harder the liquor forces fought, the harder Billy Sunday preached, and the more men climbed on the "water wagon." Pittsburgh had proved that the "East" was no different than the "West." Both were filled with men and women who needed God and would respond when Billy held out his hand and gave the invitation, "Come, come to Jesus."

12

Preaching to the Bleachers

"Whisky is all right in its place—but its place is in hell."

"The bars of the church are so low that any old hog with two or three suits of clothes and a bank roll can crawl through."

"I'm going to preach until hell freezes over, and then I'm going to get a pair of skates and keep on soaking it into Satan."

It was words like that from the preaching of Billy Sunday which made people predict he would never make it in the East. People in New York; Washington, D. C.; and Boston, Massachusetts, were dignified and civilized. They would never stand for such language.

In fact, many of the ministers themselves felt that it would be a mistake to bring Sunday into Philadelphia or New York City. When the pastors in Pittsburgh first invited him to come, the criticism was loud. Even some of the very pastors who issued the invitation began to wonder what they had done when Billy came to town for an organizational meeting and told them that most preachers were "fudge-eating mollycoddles." As for professors in theological seminaries, the thing to do to them was to "stand them on their heads in mud puddles."

But there was a reason Billy talked the way he did. For years people had associated religion with the "thee's" and "thou's" of the old Puritans, and with the "holy tones" of modern-day preachers. That meant religion had nothing to do with everyday life, because no one talked in theological terms outside of church. Billy wanted to change all that. He wanted religion to be as much a part of everyday life as baseball. And that meant he had to talk to people where they lived.

Some of the critics claimed that Billy used such language to get the attention of the newspapers. One critic wrote that "throughout his preaching, and indeed, his praying, he uses every vulgarity and ir- reverence of language, addressing his hearers and the Almighty in the idiom of the saloon, the gutter, and the yellow newspaper."

"He makes religion the sensation of the hour," claimed another critic. "His sacreligious quips are echoed in the yellow newspapers, for whom he makes the best pious copy. He has given to the gospel an immense publicity of a kind it never enjoyed before. How, then, can those interested in the spread of Chris- tianity fail to rejoice at the marvel of thousands of peo- ple who will not go to church, thronging to hear Mr. Sunday tell them about the religion of Christ in the language and with the reverence of a newsboy or a longshoreman."

It was true that Billy attracted the attention of the newspapers. When he came to town the newspapers

often carried his messages word for word. The Pittsburgh dailies published a special, "Sunday Edition."
From the building of the tabernacle to the unorthodox
language of his sermons and prayers, and then on to
the stories of the lives who were changed through his
preaching, the story was repeated in detail.

The reaction to such publicity was totally different,
depending on who was reading. Some people read the
stories and rushed to the tabernacle to hear for
themselves. Others without ever going to hear him
for themselves, charged him with being intolerant and
even violent. They criticized him for making himself
rich in the business of evangelism, for a lack of "real"
religion in the tabernacle services, and especially for
his preaching to the bleachers.

"Every day he mounts the judgment seat of the
universe and sends men by the scores to the right hand
and to the left—mostly to the left," wrote a Boston
minister, Dr. Washington Gladden. "Statistics of a
sort were kept of the number of conversions; but of
the number of those sent to hell by name, no record,
I believe, was made. It is a great omission; for that
is a large part of the business. All evolutionists are
consigned to hell. Mr. Sunday names, one by one,
those whom he supposes to be evolutionists, and with
a dramatic gesture flings each of them into perdition.
'There goes old Darwin! He's in hell sure!' And the
enraptured audience yells its applause, as one evolu-
tionist after another is dropped into the fiery pit. A
staid Methodist preacher, who watched this perform-
ance, said afterward. 'I would never have believed
it, had I not seen it, that an audience of civilized
Americans could show such a spirit as that.' The scene
at a Spanish bullfight is really, when you think of it,
less horrible."

Billy had his own answers for such criticism. If he

heard that one of the supporting preachers in a campaign was questioning his use of slang, he was likely
to turn around during a sermon, point him out in his
seat on the platform, shake his fist in his face and tell
him he was a "weak-kneed, spineless compromiser
who needed some spiritual vim, vigor, and tabasco
sauce."

If a criticism was from outside, Billy preached on
his favorite Bible preacher, John the Baptist.

"John the Baptist wasn't that kind of preacher.
John the Baptist opened the Bible right in the middle
and preached the Word of God just as he found it,
and he didn't care whether people liked it or not. That
wasn't his business. I tell you, John the Baptist stirred
up the devil. If any minister doesn't believe in the
devil, it's because he has never preached a sermon
on repentance, or he'd have heard him roar.

"The object of the Church is to cast out devils. The
devil has more sense than a lot of preachers. I have
been unfortunate enough to know D.D.'s and L.L.D's
sitting around whittling down the doctrine of the per-
sonality of the devil to as fine a point as they know
how. You are a fool to listen to them. The devil is
no fool; he is a four-flusher. He said to Christ, 'if you
are God, act like it; if you are a man, and believe the
Scriptures, act as one who believes.'

"I'll preach against any minister who is preaching
false doctrines. I don't give a rap who he is. I'll turn
my guns loose against him, and don't you forget it.

"We got a bunch of preachers breaking their necks
to please a lot of old society dames. Some ministers
say, 'If you don't repent, you'll die and go to a place,
the name of which I can't pronounce.' I can. You'll
go to hell. If some preachers were as true to their trust
as John the Baptist, they might be turned out to grass,
but they'd lay up treasures for themselves in Heaven."

One of the favorite articles written during the course of a Billy Sunday campaign was a list of all the memorable sayings from the evangelist. Reporters wrote down those sayings that caused the audience to laugh or gasp or cry, and then printed them as samples of what the evangelist was preaching. Sometimes he was incorrectly quoted, and sometimes the words sounded far worse when printed than when he spoke them. In fact, the committee in Scranton, Pennsylvania, put up posters all over the city which read:

BE FAIR!

DON'T JUDGE BILLY SUNDAY UNTIL YOU

HAVE HEARD HIM YOURSELF.

NO REPORT, VERBAL OR PRINTED, CAN

DO HIM PERFECT JUSTICE.

But still the sayings and the sermons were printed. And God used them to reach many people who never made it to the tabernacle to hear Billy in person. One letter even arrived from China, telling how an American newspaper had shown up in the interior of that country. A young Chinese boy who had studied English in school read the message and accepted Christ as Savior.

The words of Billy Sunday echoed through the bleachers around the world, calling men and women to Christ. And none of the criticism bothered him at all. He would just explain, "I want people to know what I mean, and that's why I try to get it down where they live. What do I care if some puff-eyed, dainty little dibbly-dibbly preacher goes tibbly-tibbling around because I use plain Anglo-Saxon words.

"If a man goes to hell he ought to be there, or he wouldn't be there. I believe that cards and dancing are doing more to damn the spiritual life of the Church than the grog-shops—though you can't accuse me of being a friend of that stinking, dirty, rotten, hell-soaked business.

"Some persons think they have to look like a hedgehog to be pious.

"Some homes need a hickory switch a good deal more than they do a piano.

"You can't measure manhood with a tape line around the biceps.

"If you put a polecat in the parlor, you know which will change first—the polecat or the parlor?

"When you quit living like the devil, I will quit preaching that way.

"A saloon-keeper and a good mother don't pull on the same rope.

"The reason you don't like the Bible, you old sinner, is because it knows all about you.

"Going to church doesn't make a man a Christian, any more than going to a garage makes him an automobile.

"God likes a little humor, as is evidenced by the fact that he made the monkey, the parrot—and some of you people.

"Wouldn't this city be a great place to live in if some people would die, get converted, or move away?

"Give your face to God and he will put a shine on it.

"Temptation is the devil looking through the keyhole. Yielding is opening the door and inviting him in."

13

For God
and Country

After Billy's success in Pittsburgh the invitations flowed in. Philadelphia, Boston, Baltimore, and Washington, D.C.—all wanted Sunday to come. On January 18, 1915, President Woodrow Wilson received him at the White House, and Billy spoke at the Convention Hall on "If Christ Came to Washington." Champ Clark, the Speaker of the House, introduced Billy and announced that he would be coming back in a few months to hold a full-fledged campaign, tabernacle and all.

But it was New York City where Billy really wanted to go. New York City was called the "evangelist's graveyard." The city had not experienced a revival of any kind since Dwight L. Moody and Ira B. Sankey had been there almost forty years before. To Billy it was a challenge almost as great as facing an undefeated professional baseball team. So when an invitation came from Rev. I. M. Haldeman and a committee of over one hundred other pastors, Billy accepted without any hesitation.

"We're going to build the biggest tabernacle and hold the longest meeting and see the most souls saved of any place we've ever been," he confided to Ma. The twelve-week campaign was scheduled to begin on April 8, 1917, but preparations began almost a year before that date.

John D. Rockefeller, Sr., donated a lot on the corner of Broadway and 168th Street, and the work on the tabernacle began. Seven thousand cottage prayer meetings were held with the total attendance climbing to over one hundred thousand people who met to pray for the coming revival meeting. Pledges were taken in the cooperating churches to help pay for the building. Choir members were recruited until over 6,700 people were ready to sing. The singers had to be divided into three choirs since the choir loft would hold only two thousand. Tali Esen Morgan trained the choir and then turned it over to Homer Rodeheaver when he arrived in town.

On Sunday, April 1, with the construction almost completed, the tabernacle was dedicated. Governor Whitman was present and spoke highly of the work Billy Sunday had done around the country. "I am not very much concerned about the theology of Mr. Sunday," he said. "It is enough for me and you to know that in scores of cities he has lifted thousands out of the mire of selfishness and sin, and turned their faces toward the stars." Sixteen thousand people cheered and prayed and looked forward to the arrival of Mr. Sunday himself.

But there were other forces at work in the country that same week. The European continent had been embroiled in a war for several years. After carefully maintaining the neutrality of the United States during his first term in office, it appeared that President Woodrow Wilson would soon be calling on the country to declare war on Germany. Almost two years earlier the president had protested the sinking of the *Lusitania* by German U-Boats and had been successful in getting the Kaiser to call off the submarine campaign. But since February of 1917, Germany had declared unrestricted submarine warfare against any and all shipping delivering to Europe

On April 2 President Wilson delivered his message as expected, calling on Congress to declare war. All that week the congressmen debated and then began to vote. At 3:00 A.M. on the morning of April 6 the final votes were counted. The Senate voted 82-1 and the House 373-50 to support the president. Saturday morning President Wilson made it official with his proclamation of war, and suddenly the entire nation was plunged into the frenzy of preparing for a major conflict thousands of miles from their shores.

Saturday afternoon at 5:28 P.M. Evangelist and Mrs. Billy Sunday arrived at the railroad station in New York City to give the devil his due. It was an entirely different battle that he would be waging, but he was not one to ignore the implications of a nation plunged into war. His opening address the next day was called, "God's Grenadiers."

"Service to our beloved country in war," Billy shouted as he unfurled an American flag and waved it over his head, "is equivalent to loyalty to God."

That was as far as he got. The vast crowd of over twenty thousand people which filled the tabernacle rose to their feet, cheering and shouting. It took almost five minutes before Billy could be heard again. But he did not mind. He just stood back and grinned as New York City welcomed him. When the noise finally subsided so that he could be heard, he began again.

"I tell you, good Christian people, that with the Holy Spirit there is no power on earth or in hell that can stand before the church of Jesus Christ. They've raised $500,000 here in New York City to stop me. But nothing is going to stop this meeting. The damnable, hell-born, whisky-soaked, hog-jowled, beetle-browed, peanut-brained, weasel-eyed, bull-necked, rum-soaked moral assassins have run this community long enough."

The roar that shook the wooden ceiling of the tabernacle again made it impossible even for Billy's foghorn voice be heard. So again he stood still and beamed as the crowd cheered his attack on the liquor industry. But then it was business as usual.

Running and leaping and twisting and turning, shouting and screaming and whispering, he challenged them to patriotism and loyalty to God, home, and native land. He called on the young men in the

audience to enlist, and told the girls that they should
not even consider a proposal for marriage until they
had seen the young man's enlistment papers.

For over an hour he preached, all the time running
or sliding across the platform. At one point he even
climbed up on the top of the grand piano and challenged the devil to go ten rounds with him. When he
roared, the people roared in response. When he
laughed they laughed, and when he cried they cried.
And then, just as suddenly as he had begun, the sermon was over and Billy was praying. But most of the
people did not even close their eyes because Billy's
prayers were just talks with God. Not everyone was
sure when he had even started the prayer.

"There are some dandy folks here in New York
City, lots of good men and women who are with us
in this campaign, and Lord, we want You to help
make this a great meeting. Lord, it's great to see them
pouring in like they did here today. God, You have
the people of the homes tell their maids to go to the
meeting at the Y.M.C.A. Thursday afternoon, and
God, let's have a crowd of the children at their meeting
next Saturday. Rody is going to talk to them, Lord.
He can't preach and I can't sing, but the children will
have a big time with him, Lord. Lord, I won't try
to stop people from roasting and scoring me. I would
not know what to do if I didn't get some cracks from
people now and then. Oh, Lord, bend over the battle-
ments of glory and hear the cry of old New York.
Lord, save tens of thousands of souls in this old city.
Help us, Lord, and we'll win this whisky-soaked, vice-
ridden old city of New York and lay it at Your feet."

With that unconventional prayer the service was
over. Had he invited people to hit the sawdust trail
that evening, probably everyone in the building would
have come. But it was his practice not to give an

invitation until almost two weeks into a campaign. In that way a great deal of interest was stirred as to when the first trail hitters would be called on to come. And that also gave time for him to stir up the Christians so they would go out and bring their unsaved friends to the meeting.

The first invitation during the New York campaign came on the second Friday night of the meeting. As Billy concluded his message he called, "How many of you men and women will jump to your feet and come down and say,'Bill, here's my hand for God, for home, for my native land, to live and conquer for Christ'? Come on!"

An opening had been built in the front of the platform of the New York tabernacle so that Billy could stand there and greet those who hit the trail. Soon they were shaking his hand at the rate of eighty-three a minute, and before the evening was over more than two thousand people had come to the front to shake his hand and take their stand for Christ. It was the largest group of first-night trail-hitters in any campaign Billy had ever held.

Before the twelve weeks in New York City were over, Billy's prediction to Ma had come true. Nearly one hundred thousand people in all had hit the sawdust trail. The expenses of the campaign were met early and the last day the people of the city took a free will offering for Sunday which came to an astounding $124,600. Because of the extensive work the Red Cross and the Y.M.C.A. were doing for the war effort, he gave the entire amount to these two organizations.

That fall another great campaign was held in the nation's capital. During the same time, the Congress of the United States approved and submitted to the states an amendment to the Constitution calling for prohibition of the manufacture, sale, and transportation of intoxicating beverages. The resolution was submitted to the state legislatures on December 2, 1917. Just over one year later, thirty-six states had ratified the amendment and it became the law of the land on January 16, 1919.

Billy had not only taken New York City for Christ, he had also been instrumental in bringing about the death knell for his old enemy Booze.

14

Rounding the Bases

In later years the story went around that Billy had quit baseball because it got too hard for him. The people who told that story never saw the games that went on every summer at Winona Lake, Indiana, where Billy and his family made their home.

"Come on, Rody, we need a catcher," Billy would shout, and Homer Rodeheaver would head for the ball field, "rainbow" tie and all. The uniforms were somewhat strange because most of the ministers on the grounds for Bible conference had not brought anything but their Sunday suits. But soon suit coats came off and ties were loosened as Billy organized them all into two teams.

It was practically a foregone conclusion whose team would win. Give him the worst players on the entire grounds, and Billy would lead them to victory, just on the strength of his boisterous enthusiasm. And when he got up to bat, the entire outfield headed for the back fence.

Billy's enthusiasm for preaching remained just as

strong as his love for baseball. Whether the crowd that faced him was from midwestern Des Moines, Iowa, or western Portland, Oregon, he would swing for the bleachers. Whether they were corn country "hayseeds" like himself, or college students from the great Eastern universities, the message was the same.

The Bible colleges across the nation used Billy Sunday regularly and he loved to preach to preacher boys. But the real excitement came with the visits to schools such as the University of Pennsylvania. The audience there was definitely not the "home town crowd," but it was still mighty unusual for Billy to "strike out."

Billy went to the University of Pennsylvania at the personal invitation of Provost Edgar Smith. Though he was to be there one day only, the Christian students on campus made preparations as if he were conducting a month-long campaign. Student prayer groups met for weeks in advance. Tickets were printed so that admission could be controlled, and all the tickets for the three services were spoken for before the evangelist ever arrived on campus.

Even with the ticket system, students crowded in until many young men were sitting on window sills and the rafters of the gymnasium. Over ten thousand students heard Billy preach during the course of the day.

Billy didn't mince any words just because he was facing a bunch of intellectuals. After all, you always pitch the hardest to the best hitters. He spoke to them on the subject, "What Shall I Do with Jesus?"

"This question is just as pertinent to the world today as it was to Pilate," he told them. "Pilate should have been influenced by his wife's dream. She may have been one of those miserable, pliable, plastic, two-faced, two-by-four, lick-spittle, toot-my-own-horn sort of women. But Pilate should have heeded her warning and set Jesus free.

"I have no use for the fellow who sneers and mocks at Jesus Christ. If the world is against Christ, I am against the world, with every tooth, nail, bit of skin, hair follicle, muscular molecule, articulation joint." Billy paused as he realized the crowd was enjoying the mouthful of words and beginning to laugh. He let the laughter build some and then delivered his final punch. "Yes, and even my vermiform appendix." The students knew Billy had consulted his medical dictionary just for them and roared their approval in laughter and applause.

As soon as the laughter started to subside he began again, now in complete control of the crowd. "But Pilate was just one of those rat-hole, pin-headed, pliable, standpat, free-punch, pie-counter politicans. He was the direct result of the machine gang in Jewish politics, and he was afraid that if he released Christ he would lose his job. Say, boys," and Billy leaned so far over the edge of the platform that the fellows in the front row got ready to catch him. "Are you fellows willing to slap Jesus Christ in the face in order to have someone come up and slap you on the back and say you are a good fellow and a dead-game sport? That is the surest way to lose out in life. I am giving you the experience of a life that knows.

"Pilate had his chance and he missed it. His name rings down through the ages in scorn and contempt, because he had not the courage to stand up for his convictions and Jesus Christ. Aren't you boys doing the same thing? You are convinced that Jesus Christ is the Son of God, but you are afraid of the horse-laugh the boys will give you. I don't care whether you have brains enough to fill a hogshead, or little enough to fill a thimble, you are up against this proposition. You must begin to measure Christ by the rules of God instead of the rules of men. Put Him in the God class

instead of in the man class; judge Christ by His task
and the work He performed, and see if He was only
a man.''

At the close of the service that evening, over one
thousand students rose to their feet in answer to Billy's
invitation to come to Christ. The next week one of
the seniors wrote to the school newspaper and said,
''Mr. Sunday awoke in me a realization of my evil
practices and sins so forcefully that I am going to make
a determined effort to give them up and to make
amends for the past.'' The conclusion of everyone was
that Billy had scored high at the University of
Pennsylvania.

But in another area Billy didn't score so high. When
his meetings had started back in Garner, Iowa, Billy
had traveled alone, leaving Nell and the children in
Chicago. Then for a time they had all traveled, but
that became impossible when the children were school
age. Still, Billy felt as if he needed Nell, or as he
affectionately called her, ''Ma,'' to manage the great
tabernacle campaigns that were beginning. And Ma
felt as if Billy needed her. He had a real tendency to
go too hard, to play every day as if it was his last strikeout. So the decision was made that she would travel
with him and leave the children at home with her
parents. Later the Sundays bought the home in
Winona Lake, Indiana, and left the children there with
a housekeeper while Mrs. Sunday and Billy were
gone, often for two or three months.

While the children were growing up, the arrange-
ment seemed to work out fine. The housekeeper and
the governess took care of their physical needs, made
sure they were dressed well, ate proper meals and were
in school regularly. But while Billy and Ma were out
ministering to thousands of others' spiritual needs no
one ministered to the spiritual needs of their children.

After Billy's death, Ma advised a young evangelist and his wife to avoid their experience in that area at all cost, but by that time it was already too late for their own family.

Helen, their first child, had always been quite weak. Although she grew up and lived a godly Christian life, she died quite young, which brought grief to Ma and Billy. But of the four children, she was the only one who did not bring them grief in another way.

For years Billy gave his life to preaching against booze. George, his oldest boy, moved to California as soon as he could leave home and began immediately a life of heavy drinking. Tragedy struck at a wild party he was attending when he fell to his death from a seventh-floor apartment. A telegram bearing the tragic news was handed to Billy just as he was ready to step onto the platform to preach.

Billy opened the telegram, read the message, then carefully placed it into his pocket and preached as powerfully as he had ever preached in his life.

Paul also moved to California and became a test pilot. He was killed when the plane he was testing crashed into a hill outside Burbank.

Bill, Jr., followed the example of his older brother George instead of that of his father. The newspaper reports of his boozing even in the middle of the Prohibition era followed Billy from city to city as he preached across the country. And then they received word that early one morning when he was speeding away from an all-night party in Palm Springs, the car he was driving hit a telephone pole and Billy, Jr., was killed instantly.

What the liquor forces had not been able to do to Billy, they did to his family. Though he had turned thousands away from the evil and destruction of alcohol, the bottle had reached around behind and touched his own family with tragedy.

During the 1920's there was another force that conspired against the great revival activity Billy had experienced earlier in the century. In his own words, "The liberals were coming in and taking over all the churches." There had been a time when Billy could come to a town and almost every preacher would rally behind him and promote the meeting. But the 1920's saw a change in that. More and more it was only some of the ministers who would welcome him, while others promoted what was called the "social gospel." And so the large city-wide campaigns were gradually discontinued.

Billy spoke more often in smaller towns, and his meetings lasted for a week instead of eight to twelve weeks. Thus it was that in the last five years of his life he spoke in as many towns as he had during the previous fifteen years. He moved with Mrs. Sunday to Hood River Valley in Oregon, and from there they continued to travel across the country, preaching and always calling men and women to "come to Jesus." Harry Clarke, who traveled with him as song leader after Homer Rodeheaver left to start his publishing business, told how even when three to four hundred people would respond to the invitation, Billy would return to a room behind the platform and weep and pray, "Oh that more would have come." His love for people drove him constantly to a greater work for God.

15

Home Run
to Heaven

"I've got just as much ginger and tabasco sauce for God as ever," Billy shouted to a packed church in New York City. It had been over twelve years since his great New York City campaign, and Billy was now almost seventy years old. The only thing that kept him from running and sliding across the platform was the necessity of staying in front of a microphone so the message could be broadcast over radio station WOR. But even the microphone did not keep him from climbing on a chair during the invitation to come forward.

Though the large city-wide campaigns had slowed down after the great meeting in New York City, Billy did not lack for places to preach. Large churches, small churches, summer camp meetings at Winona Lake Conference Grounds in Indiana, and even an occasional tabernacle campaign kept him and Ma and the rest of the team as busy as before.

He was also kept busy fighting the liquor forces. Instead of simply obeying the new law prohibiting alcoholic beverages, the brewers and rum-runners had gone underground. Throughout the thirteen years Prohibition was the law of the land, the criminal element in society fought the government men by making illegal whisky or smuggling it in from Canada and Jamaica in the Caribbean. So instead of shelving his sermon of "Booze," Billy had to rewrite it in order to continue the fight against illegal liquor.

But he was not content just to preach against it. During a meeting north of Memphis, Tennessee, he accompanied Sheriff Will Knight on a raid of one of the illegal whisky stills operating in that county.

"The last thing Ma said to me was, 'Don't get shot, Daddy,' " Billy Sunday related to the sheriff as they bounced down a dirt road in a Lincoln.

"You'll be in the front line, but we won't let you get shot," the sheriff replied.

"I'm not afraid of getting shot," answered Billy. "Just lead me to those peanut-brained, hog-jowled, bull-necked lobsters and I'll show you how scared I am. If I'm afraid of anything, I'm afraid of this road." The car skittered down a hill, scraped a tree, and slithered back onto the road.

"Aw, we'll get them all right," the sheriff assured him. "We got a sure-enough hot tip on this still. We're pretty near there, too."

They drove around the base of the hill. Through a gap in the paw-paw bushes they could see the barn in which the still was supposed to be located. As they rolled along, watching the barn, nothing moved. The sheriff had his gun ready, but no one interfered as they drove right up to the doors of the barn.

"I'll cover the barn in case they try to escape," one of the deputies volunteered.

"All right," agreed Sheriff Knight. "Rev. Sunday, you come with me."

Throwing open the barn doors the two men stepped inside, Sheriff Knight with his rifle held high. But still no one moved. The place was soundless. The sunbeams which could find their way through the cracks fell on a fifty-gallon copper still. There was the big boiler out of which rose a worm-pipe that bent in cork-screw coils through a cooling barrel. And along the walls were rows of barrels, covered with hemp sacks, and all full of moonshine.

Billy stood for a moment looking at all that whisky, just waiting to be sold so it could destroy families and ruin men's lives. And then he went to work. With both hands he picked up glass gallon jugs and hurled them against the wall. Someone handed him an axe and he set upon the barrels.

"Good exercise," he shouted to the sheriff as he

cracked open barrel after barrel and let the illegal booze soak the dirt floor of the barn.

Then the men built a bonfire and burned everything that would burn, barrel-staves and hoops and all. The still itself was tied on the front of the Lincoln for evidence.

When the sheriff and Billy drove back into Memphis it was almost like a parade. People stood on every corner to watch the car go by, on which was tied the copper still on the front. And that evening nearly ten thousand people came to the closing service of the Billy Sunday campaign, with thousands of them hitting the sawdust trail when the invitation was given.

In 1935, by the time he was seventy-three, Billy had spoken in person to over eighty-five million people and had seen one million of them receive Christ as Savior. His sawdust trail had reached into every state of the union. And he was still preaching. The Sunday before he died he traveled to Mishawaka, Indiana, to preach in the church where Homer Rodeheaver was serving as choir leader. The auditorium was crowded with people, some sitting on the platform, and even on the piano.

But it was obvious to Ma and others that Billy was on third base just waiting for an opportunity to go home, home to Heaven. He had experienced several heart attacks, and more than once during the last three years he had found it necessary to cancel engagements due to illness. Many times Nell had sat in the ballpark and cheered as Billy rounded third and dashed home to be called "safe" by the umpire. Now she sat and watched again as he rounded third heading toward Heaven.

It was on a Wednesday, November 6, 1935, that Billy suffered what was to be the fatal heart attack.

The family doctor lived right next door and came quickly at Ma's request.

After an examination he rose to leave. "Mr. Sunday, your pulse is much better, but I'll be back to check on you at eight o'clock."

"Well, Doc," Billy managed, "will I be up and preaching again by Sunday?"

The doctor could not answer, but put up his fingers making a "V" for victory.

"You won't forget me now, will you, Doc?"

"I won't. I couldn't forget you if I wanted to, Mr. Sunday."

Billy lay back on the pillow and seemed comfortable. Ma began to read to him from a stack of letters which had arrived. Then she heard Billy call, "Ma, I'm dizzy." And with that the baseball evangelist headed home.

Several years before, Billy had preached a message in which he imagined what it would be like to step into Heaven. He said the first thing he wanted to do was shake hands with Jesus.

"Jesus, thank You. I'm glad You honored me with salvation. I'm glad You honored me with the privilege of preaching your gospel. And now, Jesus, I'd like to see my old Aunty Griffith.

"Hello, Granny. I just left earth last night. You say you live right next door to my mom? Good, Granny! I knew the Lord would let you in.

"Howdy do, Isaac. Where is Jacob?

"Hello, Joseph. Say old man, that was a rough deal they tried to put over on you down there in Egypt, when the woman tried to tempt you and you looked her square in the eye and pushed her away. Say, Joseph, I like you.

"Where's Peter, and James, and John, and Andrew, and Philip? I want to see them all.

"And then I looked around and saw the sun in all
its regal splendor and said to the people, 'When will
the sun set?' I looked at their splendid clothing and
said, 'When are the working men clad in overalls?
Where are the brawny men who toil? And they
answered, 'We toil not, for there remaineth a rest for
the people of God.'

"I looked upon glistening towers and spires, but
found no tombstones or mausoleums. I said, 'Where
are the hearses that carry your dead? Where are
undertakers that embalm the dead?' The reply came
again, 'We never die in this land.'

"Then I strolled along and heard the ripple of water
as waves broke against the jeweled beach. I saw boats
with bows of gold and with oars tipped with silver.
I saw multitudes that no man could number. We
crossed green meadows sweet with violets and
varicolored flowers. The air pulsed with the music of
songbirds. And they caroled and sang my welcome,
and we went leaping and shouting with glee, 'Home—
Home—Home!

"Finally I approached Jesus, who had first welcomed me into the heavenly places. 'Say, Jesus,' I
said, 'could I hang around the gate awhile, to welcome
the rest of my family in? Thanks, Jesus.'

"Say, don't let God hang a 'For Rent' sign on your
mansion above. Send word to Him that you want that
place. Come down here and take my hand and tell
God you're coming. Eternal life is the underlying
desire of everybody. But you can't buy it. It's a gift
of God. By His grace, I have salvation through Jesus
Christ, and I wouldn't trade it for a deed to the whole
world.''

"Hello, Helen. Hey, George. Hey, Will. Hey, little
Paul. Come on in.''

Dr. Harry Ironside, pastor of Moody Memorial

Church in Chicago, offered his church for Billy's funeral service. Hundreds of ministers filled the choir loft. Flowers came from many people, including the Chicago White Stockings team, with whom Billy had been playing at the time of his conversion.

Harry Clarke, who had traveled with the Sundays for several years after Homer Rodeheaver left, sang "God's Tomorrow." And Homer Rodeheaver himself sang "Good-Morning Up There."

Dr. Timothy Stone, a Presbyterian minister from Chicago who had been present when Billy Sunday was ordained, brought one of the messages.

"This service cannot be a day of mouring, but a day of coronation," he said. "The poet said, 'Why should it be a wrench/To leave your wooden bench?/Why not with happy shout,/run home when school is out?'

"Few men have been welcomed home to Heaven by more than he. Since the unique Christ-like Moody, in whose memorial church we bow today, there has been no greater soulwinner among American citizens.

"Billy Sunday loved people and longed to introduce them to the best Friend he and mankind ever had, Jesus Christ. Rich and poor, high and low, prince and pauper, drunkard and harlot, he loved and welcomed in the name of the Lowly Man of Nazareth."

Next Harry Clarke rose to lead the congregation in the great song which had become a trademark of the Sunday campaigns. "You know, people," he began, "I have heard Mr. Sunday say many times that when it came to the time of his leaving earth, he didn't want a sad meeting. He would say constantly, 'If ever I leave this place in a hurry, there is one song I want you to be sure to have the people sing,' and if he were here, he would prompt us and say, 'Let's get away from the black crepe and sing the Glory

Song.' The finest tribute we could pay to Mr. Sunday would be to sing:

> When all my labors and trials are o'er,
> And I am safe on that beautiful shore.

"Mr. Sunday is safe. I would like to impose on Mr. Rodeheaver; he has been with him for many years, and Mr. Sunday would be glad to have him sing it."

And with the two great songleaders singing the way, the audience followed.

> When all my labors and trials are o'er,
> And I am safe on that beautiful shore,
> Just to be near the dear Lord I adore,
> Will through the ages be glory for me.

> (*Chorus*) Oh, that will be glory for me!
> Glory for me! Glory for me!
> When by His grace I shall look on His face,
> That will be glory, be glory for me!

> Friends will be there I have loved long ago:
> Joy like a river around me will flow;
> Yet, just a smile from my Savior I know
> Will through the ages be glory for me.

Tears mingled strangely with shouts of joy as the vast congregation sang together the beloved words.

Then Dr. Harry Ironsides, pastor of Moody Memorial Church, said, "It was through the Pacific Garden Mission, as you know, that Mr. Sunday was led to a knowledge of the Lord Jesus Christ, so it seems most fitting that we should have with us today the Rev. Walter Taylor, now Superintendent of the Pacific Garden Mission, who will pronounce the benediction."

After the prayer the crowd lined up again to take a final look at America's baseball evangelist.

A preacher from Buffalo, New York, approached Mrs. Sunday at the funeral service. "Mrs. Sunday," he said, "I have never been to a funeral service quite like this. Why, it's like a great revival service. The glory songs have all been sung. All the preachers have been up there pleading with sinners to come down and be saved. Why, I understand that a man was converted just walking through the line to get a glimpse of your husband in the casket yesterday. I think this is just the kind of funeral your husband would have wanted."

Ma Sunday smiled. She knew it was the type of service Billy wanted because they had talked it over and planned it together. Billy wanted to be just as much a soulwinner in his death as he had been in his life. But they hadn't talked over or even considered what the minister asked next.

"Mrs. Sunday, do you suppose you could come to my church in Buffalo, New York, for another memorial service for Billy? We have thousands of people in our town who would have loved to come here to Chicago today and just couldn't make the trip. We would like to have a memorial service in our church and would like you to be there if at all possible."

At first Ma hesitated. She had traveled with Billy for years, but never to do any speaking. But then she remembered a prayer she had voiced when Billy was dying. "Lord," she had prayed, "if there's anything left in the world for me to do, You let me know."

"When?" she asked the preacher.

"Well, I was thinking about a week from Tuesday. I realize that doesn't give you a very long time to make arrangements, and with the funeral today and all—"

But Ma Sunday wasn't listening, she was counting the days. "That would be November 19. Do you know what day that is?"

"Well, no. But if there is a conflict we could set a better time."

"There is no better time," replied Ma with determination. "November 19 is Billy's birthday. I would be pleased to come."

So just ten days after Billy's memorial service at the Moody Memorial Church in Chicago, Ma Sunday got off the train in Buffalo, New York, for another memorial service. As the train slowed to a halt she could hear the newsboys shouting on the platform, "Extra! Extra! Read all about it. Billy Sunday's first birthday in Heaven." The *Buffao Courier* had run a double streamer headline in bold two-inch letters, "Billy Sunday's First Birthday in Heaven." A subtitle read, "Nell Sunday to Address Memorial Service Tonight."

It had been almost twenty years since Billy had visited the city of Buffalo, but people had not forgotten. From there Nell was invited to another city in New York, and from there the invitations came from across the nation. Right up until her death in 1956 the Lord let her know that there certainly was something "left in the world for her to do." Countless "preacher boys" in Bible schools who had never heard her husband preach were challenged to blaze their own trails for Christ because of her vivid memories of the sawdust trail.

And so the life of Billy Sunday ended. His body was laid in the beautiful Forest Park Cemetery in Chicago and marked by a ten-foot granite stone. The verse, "I have fought a good fight, I have finished my course, I have kept the faith" (II Timothy 4:7) was inscribed upon it. Under the verse is an open Bible.

But what would have pleased Billy the most were the more than seven thousand common people—

railroad men, store clerks, maids, and steel workers—
who filed past the casket for one last look at the man
who had such a great influence in their lives. Hundreds of them were heard to say as they filed past,
"He led me to Christ." The sawdust trail had ended,
but the results would continue on for all eternity.

Events in the Life of
Billy Sunday

1861, Feb. - Confederate States of America established.

1862, July - William Ashley Sunday enlists in the Twenty-third Iowa Infantry Volunteers.

1862, Nov. 19 - William Ashley Sunday, Jr., is born.

1862, Dec. 22 - William Ashely Sunday, Sr., dies of pneumonia in the service in Patterson, Missouri.

1865, April 9 - General Robert E. Lee surrenders to General U. S. Grant.

1869, Spring - Cincinnati Red Stockings begin to pay their players and so become the first professional baseball team.

1873, Fall - Ed and Billy Sunday are sent to the Soldiers' Orphans' Home in Glenwood, Iowa.

1875, Spring - The boys are transferred to the home in Davenport.

1876, June - Ed and Billy leave the orphanage and return home.

1876, Summer - Eight professional baseball teams form the National League.

1876, Fall - Rutherford B. Hayes wins a hotly contested election over Samuel J. Tilden to become President.

1881, July 2 - President James A. Garfield is shot by an assassin.

1881, Sept. 19 - President Garfield dies of his gunshot wounds.

1883, Spring - Billy Sunday joins 'Cap' Anson and the Chicago White Stockings team.

1884 - President Grover Cleveland becomes the first Democrate elected President since the Civil War.

1886 - The Chicago White Stockings lose the first world championship of baseball to the St. Louis Browns.

1887, Fall - Billy Sunday accepts Christ as Savior at the Pacific Garden Mission in Chicago.

1888, Sept. 5 - Sunday marries Helen Thompson at the Jefferson Avenue Presbyterian Church in Chicago.

1890, Fall - Billy is traded from the Pittsburgh Pirates to Philadelphia and signs a three-year contract.

1891, March 17 - The Philadelphia team releases Billy from his contract and he accepts a job with the Y.M.C.A. in Chicago.

1893 - Billy resigns from the Y.M.C.A. to become the "advance" man for Evangelist J. Wilbur Chapman.

1895, Dec. - Dr. Chapman accepts the pastorate of Bethany Presbyterian church in Philadelphia and leaves evangelism.

1896, Jan. - Bill Sunday holds his first evanglistic meeting in Garner, Iowa.

1898, April 21 - Spanish-American War begins.

1901, Sept. 14 - President William McKinley is assassinated. Theodore Roosevelt becomes President.

1903, April 13 - Sunday is ordained to the gospel ministry by the Chicago presbytery.

1905 - First Billy Sunday Tabernacle is erected in Perry, Iowa.

1907 - Homer Rodeheaver becomes Sunday's song leader.

1914 - World War I begins in Europe.

1915, Jan. 18 - President Woodrow Wilson entertains Billy at the White House.

1915, Jan.-Mar - The largest Sunday campaign yet is held in Philadelphia with over two million people in attendance.

1917, April 2 - President Wilson asks Congress to declare war on Germany.

1917, April 7 - War is declared.

1917, April 8 - The twelve-week New York City campaign gets underway, nearly one hundred thousand people hit the sawdust trail before it is over.

1919, Jan. 16 - Prohibition is approved as the eighteenth amendment to the Constitution.

1920 - Warren G. Harding is elected President.

1927 - Homer Rodeheaver leaves the Billy Sunday Evangelistic Organization and is replaced by Harry Clarke.

1929, Oct. 29 - The stock market crash begins the Great Depression.

1932 - Franklin D. Roosevelt is elected President.

1933, Dec. 5 - Prohibition is repealed by the twenty-first Amendment to the Constitution.

1935, Oct. 27 - Billy Sunday preaches his last sermon in Mishawaka, Indiana.

1935, Nov. 6 - Sunday suffers a fatal heart attack and the ''sawdust trail'' is ended.

The Booze Sermon

Billy Sunday preached hundreds of times throughout the United States over a period of many years. One of his most famous sermons was ''Booze, Or, Get On the Water Wagon.'' He preached this sermon at least once a week for a period of more than thirty years. It went through several revisions before, during and after Prohibition (the time from 1920 through 1933 when it was the law in the United States that alcoholic beverages were not allowed to be sold).

Often in a town where Billy had preached this sermon, the saloons (or bars, as we would call them today) were forced to close because not enough people continued to visit them. Although the sermon remained much the same from year to year, here it is in one of its revisions.

Booze
or
Get On the Water Wagon

I will take my text from the eighth chapter of Matthew, the twenty-eighth to the thirty-second verse, describing the casting out of the devils, which entered into the swine.

Here we have one of the strangest scenes in all the Gospels. Two men, possessed of devils, confront Jesus, and while the devils are crying out for Jesus to leave them, He commands the devils to come out, and the devils obey the command of Jesus. The devils ask permission to enter into a herd of swine feeding on the hillside. This is the only record we have of Jesus ever granting the petition of devils, and He did it for the salvation of men.

Then the fellows that kept the hogs went back to town and told the peanut-brained, weasel-eyed, hog-jowled, beetle-browed, bull-necked lobsters that owned the hogs, that a "long-haired fanatic from Nazareth, named Jesus, had driven the devils out of some men and the devils have gone into the hogs, and the hogs into the sea, and the sea into the hogs, and the whole bunch is dead."

And then the fat, pussy old fellows came out to see Jesus and said that He was hurting their business. A fellow says to me, "I don't think Jesus Christ did a nice thing."

You don't know what you are talking about.

Down in Nashville, Tenn., I saw four wagons going down the street, and they were loaded with stills, and kettles, and pipes. "What's this?" I asked.

United States revenue officers, and they have been in the moonshine district and confiscated the illicit stills, and they are taking them down to the government scrap heap."

Jesus Christ was God's revenue officer. Now, the Jews were forbidden to eat pork, but Jesus Christ came and found that crowd buying and selling and dealing in pork, and confiscated the whole business, and He kept within the limits of the law when He did it. Then the fellows ran back to those who owned the hogs to tell what had befallen them and those hog-owners said to Jesus: "Take your helpers and hike. You are hurting our business." And they looked into the sea and the hogs were bottom side up, but the men were right side up. And Jesus said: "What is the matter?"

And they answered: "Leave our hogs and go." A fellow says it is rather a strange request for the devils to make, to ask permission to enter into hogs, I don't know—if I was a devil I would rather live in a good, decent hog than in lots of men and if you will drive the hog out you won't have to carry slop to him, so I will try to help you get rid of the hog.

And they told Jesus to leave the country. They said: "You are hurting our business."

"Have you no interest in manhood?"

"We have no interest in that; just take your disciples and leave, for you are hurting our business."

That is the attitude of the liquor traffic toward the church, and state, and government, and the preacher that has the backbone to fight the most damnable, corrupt institution that ever wriggled out of hell and fastened itself on the public.

I am a temperance Republican down to my toes. Who is the man that fights the whisky business in the South? It is the Democrat! They have driven the business from Alabama; they have driven it from Georgia, and from Mississippi, and Tennessee, all but three cities, and out of 100 counties in Kentucky. And they have driven it out of 147 counties in Texas, and out of North Carolina. And it is the rock-ribbed Democratic South that is fighting the saloon. They started this fight that is sweeping like fire over the United States. You might as well try and dam Niagara Falls with tooth picks as to stop the reform wave sweeping our land. The Democratic party of Florida has put a temperance plank in its platform, and the Republican party of every state would nail that plank in their platform if they thought it would carry the election. It is simply a matter of decency and manhood, irrespective of politics. It is prosperity against poverty, sobriety against drunkenness, honesty against thieving, Heaven against hell. Don't you want to see men sober? Brutal, staggering men transformed into respectable citizens? "No," said a saloonkeeper, "to hell with men. We are interested in our business, we have no interest in humanity."

After all is said that can be said upon the liquor traffic, its influence is degrading upon the individual, the family, politics and business, and upon everything that you touch in this old world. For the time has long gone by when there is any ground for arguments of its ill effects. All are agreed on that point. There is just one prime reason why the saloon has not been knocked into hell, and that is the false statement, "that the saloons are needed to help lighten the taxes." The saloon business has never paid, and it cost fifty times more for the saloon than the revenue derived from it.

I challenge you to show me where the saloon has ever helped business, education, church morals or anything we hold dear.

You listen today, and if I can't peel the bark off that damnable fallacy, I will pack my trunk and leave. I say that is the biggest lie ever belched out. . . . I defy any whisky man on God's dirt to show one town that has the saloon, where the taxes are lower than where they do not have the saloon. I defy you to show me an instance.

. . . Five Points, in New York, was a spot as near like hell as any spot on earth. There are five streets that run to this point, and right in the middle was an old brewery, and the streets on either side were lined with grogshops. The newspapers turned a searchlight on the district, and before they could stop it, the first thing they had to do was to buy the old brewery and turn it into a mission, and today it is a decent, respectable place.

The saloon is the sum of all villainies. It is worse
than war or pestilence. It is the crime of crimes, It
is the parent of crimes and the mother of sins. It is
the appalling source of misery and crime in the land,
and the principal cause of crime. It is the source of
three-fourths of the crime, and, of course, it is the
source of three-fourths of the taxes to support that
crime. And to license such an incarnate fiend of hell
is the dirtiest, low-down, damnable business on top
of this old earth. There is nothing to be compared to it.

. . . Do away with the cursed business and you will
not have to put up to support them. Who gets the
money? The saloonkeepers, and the brewers and the
distillers, while the whisky fills the land with misery,
and poverty and wretchedness, and disease and death,
and damnation, and it is being authorized by the will
of the sovereign people.

You say that "people will drink anyway." Not by
my vote. You say, "men will murder their wives
anyway." Not by my vote. "They will steal anyway."
Not by my vote. You are the sovereign people, and
what are you going to do about it?

Let me assemble before your minds the bodies of
the drunken dead, who crawl away "into the jaws of
death, into the mouth of hell," and then, out of the
valley of the shadow of the drink; let me call the
appertaining motherhood, and wifehood, and
childhood, and let their tears rain down upon their
purple faces. Do you think that would stop the curse
of the liquor traffic? No! No!

In these days when the question of saloon or no
saloon is at the fore in almost every community, one
hears a good deal about what is called "personal
liberty." These are fine, large, mouth-filling words
that certainly do sound first rate; but when you get
right down and analyze them in the light of common

old horse sense, you will discover that in their applica-
tion to the present controversy they mean just about
this: ''Personal liberty,'' is for the man who, if he has
the inclination and the price, can stand up to a bar
and fill his hide so full of red liquor that he is transformed for the time into an irresponsible, dangerous,
evil smelling brute. But ''personal liberty'' is not for
his patient, long-suffering wife, who has to endure with
what fortitude she may his blows and curses; nor is
it for his children who, if they escape his insane rage
are yet robbed of every known joy and privilege of
childhood, and too often grow up neglected, uncared
for and vicious as the result of their surroundings and
the example before them. ''Personal liberty'' is not
for the sober, industrious citizen who from the pro-
ceeds of honest toil and orderly living, has to pay, will-
ingly or not, the tax bills which pile up as a direct result
of drunkenness, disorder, and poverty, the items of
which are written in the records of every police court
and poor-house in the land; nor is ''personal liberty''
for the good woman who goes abroad in the town only
at the risk of being shot down by some drink-crazed
creature. This rant about ''personal liberty'' as an
argument, has no leg to stand upon.

. . . Two years ago in the city of Chicago a young
man of good parents, good character, one Sunday
crossed the street and entered a saloon, open against
the law. He found there boon companions. There was
laughter, song and jest and much drinking. After a
while, drunk, insanely drunk, his money gone, he was
kicked into the street. He found his way across to his
mother's home. He importuned her for money to buy
more drink. She refused him. He seized from the
sideboard a revolver and ran out into the street and
with the expressed determination of entering the
saloon and getting more drink, money or no money.

His little mother followed him into the street. She put her hand upon him in a loving restraint. He struck it from him in anger and then his sister came and added her entreaty in vain. And then a neighbor, whom he knew, trusted and respected, came and put his hand on him in gentleness and friendly kindness but in an instant of drunken rage he raised the revolver and shot his friend dead in his blood upon the street. There was a trial; he was found guilty of murder. He was sentenced to life imprisonment and when the little mother heard the verdict—a frail little bit of a woman—she threw up her hands and fell in a swoon. In three hours she was dead.

In the streets of Freeport, Ill., a young man of good family became involved in a controversy with a lewd woman of the town. He went in a drunken frenzy to his father's home, armed himself with a deadly weapon and set forth the city in search of the woman with whom he had quarreled. The first person he met upon the public square in the city, in the daylight, in a place where she had a right to be, was one of the most cultured women of Freeport. She carried in her arms her babe, motherhood and babyhood, upon the streets of Freeport in the daytime where they had a right to be, but this young man in his drunken insanity mistook her for the woman he sought and shot her dead upon the streets with her babe in her arms. He was tried and Judge Ferand, in sentencing him to life imprisonment, said, "You are the seventh man in two years to be sentenced for murder while intoxicated."

In the city of Anderson, you remember the tragedy in the Blake home. A young man came home intoxicated, demanding money of his mother. She refused it. He seized from the wood box a hatchet and killed his mother, and then robbed her. You remember he fled. The officers of the law pursued him, brought him

back. And indictment was read to him, charging him
with the murder of the mother who had given him
his birth, of her who had gone down into the valley
of the shadow of death to give him life, of her who
had looked down into his blue eyes and thanked God
for his life. And he said, "I am guilty, I did it all."
And Judge McClure sentenced him to life
imprisonment.

. . . I tell you, gentlemen, the American home is
the dearest heritage of the people, for the people, by
the people and when a man can go from home in the
morning with the kisses of his wife and children on
his lips, and come back at night with an empty dinner bucket to a happy home, that man is a better man,
whether white or black. Whatever takes away the com-
forts of home—whatever degrades that man or
woman—whatever invades the sanctity of the home,
is the deadliest foe to the home, the church and the
state, on top of God Almighty's dirt. And if all the
combined forces of hell should assemble in conclave,
and with them all the men on earth that hate and
despise God, and purity, and virtue—if all the scum
of the earth could mingle with the denizens of hell to
try to think of the deadliest institution to home, to
church and state, I tell you, sir, the combined hellish
intelligence could not conceive of or bring an institution that could touch the hem of the garment of the
open licensed saloon to damn the home and manhood,
and womanhood and business and every other good
thing on God's earth.

In the island of Jamaica the rats increased so that
they destroyed the crops, and they introduced the
mongoose, which is a species of the coon. They have
three breeding seasons a year and there are 12 to 15
in each brood, and they are deadly enemies of the rats.
The result was that the rats disappeared and there was

nothing more for the mongoose to feed upon, so they attacked the snakes, and the frogs, and the lizards that fed upon the insects, with the result that the insects increased and they stripped the gardens, eating up the onions and lettuce and then the mongoose attacked the sheep, and the cats, and the geese. Now Jamaica is spending hundreds of thousands of dollars to get rid of the mongoose.

The American mongoose is the open licensed saloon. It eats the carpets off the floor, and the clothes from off your back, your money out of the bank, and it eats up character, and it goes on until at last it leaves a stranded wreck in the home, a skeleton of what was once brightness and happiness.

. . . As Dr. Howard said: "I tell you that the saloon is a coward. It hides itself behind stained glass doors, and opaque windows, and sneaks its customers in at a blind door, and it keeps a sentinel to guard the door from the officers of the law, and it marks its wares with false bills-of-lading, and offers to ship green goods to you and marks them with the names of wholesome articles of food so people won't know what is being sent to you. And so vile did that business get that the Legislature of Indiana passed a law forbidding a saloon to ship goods without being properly labeled. And the United States Congress passed a law forbidding them to send whisky through the mails.

I tell you it strikes in the night. It fights under cover of darkness and assassinates the character that it cannot damn, and it lies about you. It attacks defenseless womanhood and childhood. The saloon is a coward. It is a thief, it is not an ordinary court defender that steals your money, but it robs you of manhood and leaves you in rags and takes away your friends, and it robs your family. It impoverishes your children and it brings insanity and suicide. It will take the shirt off

your back and it will steal the coffin from a dead child
and yank the last crust of bread out of the hand of
the starving child; it will take the last bucket of coal
out of your cellar, and the last cent out of your pocket,
and will send you home bleary-eyed and staggering
to your wife and children. It will steal the milk from
the breast of the mother and leave her with nothing
with which to feed her infant. It will take the virtue
from your daughter. It is the dirtiest, most lowdown,
damnable business that ever crawled out of the pit of
hell. It is a sneak, and a thief and a coward.

It is an infidel. It has no faith in God; it has no
religion. It would close every church in the land. It
would hang its beer signs on the abandoned altars.
It would close every public school. It respects the thief
and it esteems the blasphemer; it fills the prisons and
the penitentiaries. It despises Heaven, hates love,
scorns virtue. It tempts the passions. Its music is the
song of a siren. Its sermons are a collection of lewd,
vile stories. It wraps a mantle about the home of this
world and that to come. Its tables are full of the vilest
literature. It is the moral clearing house of rot, and
damnation, and poverty, and insanity, and it wrecks
homes and blights lives today.

The saloon is a liar. It promises good cheer and
sends sorrow. It promises health and causes disease.
It promises prosperity and sends adversity. It promises
happiness and sends misery. Yes, it sends the husband home with a lie on his lips to his wife; and the
boy home with a lie on his lips to his mother; and it
causes the employee to lie to his employer. It degrades.
It is God's worst enemy and the devil's best friend.
It spares neither youth nor old age. It is waiting with
a dirty blanket for the baby to crawl into this world.
It lies in wait for the unborn.

It cocks the highwayman's pistol. It puts the rope

in the hands of the mob. It is the anarchist of the world and its dirty red flag is dyed with the blood of women and children, and it sent the bullet through the body of Lincoln; it nerved the arm that sent the bullets through Garfield and William McKinley. Yes, it is a murderer. Every plot that was ever hatched against the government and law, was born and bred, and crawled out of the grogshop to damn this country.

I tell you that the curse of God Almighty is on the saloon. Legislatures are legislating against it. Decent society is barring it out. The fraternal brotherhoods are knocking it out. The Masons and Odd Fellows, and the Knights of Pythias, and the A.O.U.W., are closing their doors to the whisky sellers. They don't want you wriggling your carcass in their lodges. Yes, sir; I tell you, the curse of God is on it. It is on the down grade. It is headed for hell, and by the grace of God, I am going to give it a push, with a whoop, for all I know how. Listen to me! I am going to show you how we burn up our money.

. . . I am John, a drunken bum, and I will spend my dollar. I have worked a week and got my pay. I go into a grogshop and throw down my dollar. The saloonkeeper gets my dollar and I get a quart of booze. Come home with me. I stagger, and reel, in my wife's presence, and she says: ''Hello, John, what did you bring home?''

''A quart.''

What will a quart do? It will burn up my happiness and my home and fill my home with squalor and want. So here is the dollar. The saloonkeeper has it. Here is my quart. There, you get the whisky end of it. Here you get the workingman's end of the saloon.

But come on; I will go to a store and spend a dollar for a pair of shoes. I want them for my son, and he puts them on his feet, and with the shoes to protect

his feet he goes out and earns another dollar, and my
dollar becomes a silver thread in the woof and warp
of happiness and joy, and the man that owns the
building gets some, and the clerk that sold the shoes
gets some, and the merchant, and the traveling man,
and the wholesale houses get some, and the factory
and the man that made the shoes, and the man that
tanned the hide, and the butcher that bought the calf,
and the farmer that raised the calf, and the little
colored fellow that shined the shoes, and my dollar
spread itself and nobody is made the worse for spending the money.

. . . Say, wife, the bread that ought to be in your
stomach to satisfy the cravings of hunger is down
yonder in the grocery store, and your husband hasn't
money enough to carry it home. The meat that ought
to satisfy your hunger hangs in the butcher shop. Your
husband hasn't many money to buy it. The cloth for
a dress is lying on the shelf in a store but your husband hasn't the money to buy it. The whisky gang
has it.

. . . Come on; I'm going to line up the drunkards.
Come on ready, forward, march, right, left, here I
come with all the drunkards. We will line up in front
of a butcher shop. The butcher says: "What do you
want, a piece of neck?"

"No; how much do I owe you?" "Three dollars."
"Here's your dough. Now give me a porterhouse
steak and a sirloin roast."

"Where did you get all that money?"

"Went to hear Bill and climbed on the water
wagon."

"Hello, what do you want?"

"Beefsteak."

"What do you want?"

"Beefsteak."

We empty the shop and the butcher runs to the telephone. "Hey, central, give me the slaughter house. Have you got any beef, any pork, any mutton?"

They strip the slaughter house and then telephone to Swift, and Armour, and Nelson Morris, and Cudahy, to send down trainloads of beefsteak.

The whole bunch has gotten on the water wagon.

And Swift and the other big packers in Chicago say to their salesmen: "Buy beef, pork and mutton."

The farmer sees the price of cattle and sheep jump up to three times their value. Let me take the money you dump into the whisky hole and buy beefsteaks with it. I will show what is the matter with America. I think the liquor business is the dirtiest, rottenest business this side of hell.

Come on, are you ready? Fall in! We line up in front of a grocery store.

"What do you want?"

"Why, I want flour."

"What do you want?"

"Flour."

"What do you want?"

"Flour."

"Pillsbury, Minneapolis, Sleepy Eye?"

"Yes, ship in trainloads of flour, send on fast mail schedule, with an engine in front, one behind and a Mogul in the middle."

"What's the matter?"

"Why, the workingmen have stopped spending their money for booze and have begun to buy flour."

The big mills tell their men to buy wheat and the farmers see the price jump to over $3 a bushel. What's the matter with the country? Why, the whisky gang has your money and you have an empty stomach, and yet you will walk up and vote for the dirty traffic.

Come on, cut out the booze, boys. Get on the water

wagon; get on for the sake of your wife and babies, and hit booze a blow.

Come on, ready, forward, march! Right, left, halt! We are in front of a dry goods store.

"What do you want?"

"Calico."

"What do you want?"

"Calico."

"What do you want?"

"Calico."

"Calico, all right, come on." The stores are stripped.

Hey, Marshal Field, Carson, Pirie Scott & Co., J. V. Farrell, send down calico. The whole bunch has voted out the saloons and we have such a demand for calico we don't know what to do. And the big stores telegraph to Fall River to ship calico, and they tell their salesmen to buy cotton, and the cotton plantation man sees cotton jump up to $150 a bale.

What is the matter? Your children are going naked and the whisky gang has got your money. That's what's the matter with you. Don't listen to these old whisky-soaked politicians who say, "Stand pat on the saloon."

Come with me. Now, remember, we have the whole bunch of booze fighters on the water wagon, and I'm going home now. Over here I was John, the drunken bum. The whisky gang got my dollar and I got the quart. Over here I am John on the water wagon. The merchant got my dollar and I have got his meat, flour and calico, and I'm going home now. "Be it ever so humble, there's no place like home without booze."

Wife comes out and says, "Hello, John, what have you got?"

"Two porterhouse steaks, Sally."

"What's that bundle, pa?"

"Cloth to make you a new dress, sis. Your mother has fixed your old one so often it looks like a crazy quilt."

"And what have you got there?"

"That's a pair of shoes for you, Tom. And here is some cloth to make you a pair of pants. Your mother has patched the old ones so often they look like the map of the United States."

What's the matter with the country? We have been dumping the money into the whisky hole that ought to have been spent for flour, beef and calico, and we haven't that hole filled up yet.

A man comes along and says: "Are you a drunkard?"

"Yes, I'm a drunkard."

"Where are you going?"

"I'm going to hell."

"Why?"

"Because the Good Book says: 'No drunkard shall inherit the kingdom of God,' so I am going to hell."

Another man comes along and I say: "Are you a church member?"

"Yes, I am a church member."

"Where are you going?"

"I am going to Heaven."

"Did you vote for the saloon?"

"Yes."

"Then you shall go to hell."

Say, if the man that drinks the whisky goes to hell, the man that votes for the saloon that sold the whisky to him will go to hell. If the man that drinks the whisky goes to hell, and the man that sold the whisky to the men that drank it, goes to Heaven, then the poor drunkard will have the right to stand on the brink of eternal damnation and put his arm around the pillar of justice, shake his fist in the face of the Almighty and say, "Unjust! Unjust!" If you vote for the dirty business you ought to go to hell as sure as you live, and would like to fire the furnace while you are there.

Some fellow says: "Drive the saloon out and the building will be empty." Which would you rather have, empty buildings, or empty jails, penitentiaries and insane asylums? You drink the stuff and what have you to say? You that vote for it, and you that sell it? Look at them painted on the canvas of your recollection.

What is the matter with this grand old country? I heard my friend, George Stuart, tell how he imagined that he walked up to a mill and said:

"Hello, there, what kind of a mill are you?"

"A sawmill."

"And what do you make?"

"We make boards out of logs."

"Is the finished product worth more than the raw material?"

"Yes."

"We will make laws for you. We must have lumber for houses."

He goes up to another mill and says:

"Hey, what kind of a mill are you?"

"A grist mill."

"What do you make?"

"Flour and meal out of wheat and corn."

"Is the finished product worth more than the raw material?"

"Yes."

"Then come on. We will make laws for you. We will protect you."

He goes up to another mill and says:

"What kind of a mill are you?"

"A paper mill."

"What do you make paper out of?"

"Straw and rags."

"Well, we will make laws for you. We must have paper on which to write notes and mortgages."

He goes up to another mill and says:

"Hey, what kind of a mill are you?"

"A gin mill."

"I don't like the looks nor the smell of you. A gin mill; what do you make? What kind of a mill are you?"

"A gin mill."

"What is your raw material?"

"The boys of America."

(At this point in his sermon, Sunday usually stopped while a troop of Boy Scouts, each carrying an American flag, marched onto the platform. The dramatic interlude never failed to make its point— Editor's Note).

The gin mills of this country must have 2,000,000 boys or shut up shop. Say, walk down your streets, count the homes and every fifth home has to furnish a boy for a drunkard. Have you furnished yours? No. Then I have to furnish two to make up.

"What is your raw material?"

"American boys."

"Then I will pick up the boys and give them to you."

A man says, "Hold on there. Not that boy. He is mine."

Then I will say to you what a saloonkeeper said to me when I protested: "I am not interested in boys; to hell with your boys."

"Say, saloon gin mill, what is your finished product?"

"Bleary-eyed, low-down, staggering men and the scum of God's dirt.

Go to the jails, to the insane asylums and the

penitentiaries, and the homes for feeble-minded.
There you will find the finished product for their dirty
business. I tell you it is the worst business this side
of hell and you know it.

"Listen! Here is an extract from the Saturday Evening Post of November 9, 1907, taken from a paper
read by a brewer. You will say that a man didn't say
it: "It appears from these facts that the success of our
business lies in the creation of appetite among the
boys. Men who have formed the habit scarcely ever
reform, but they, like others, will die, and unless there
are recruits made to take their places, our coffers will
be empty, and I recommend to you that money spent
in the creation of appetite will return in dollars to your
tills, after the habit is formed."

What is your raw material, saloons? American
boys. Say, I would not give one boy for all the distillers
and saloons this side of hell. And they have to have
2,000,000 boys every generation. And then you tell
me you are a man when you will vote for an institution like that. What do you want to do, pay taxes in
money or in boys?

I feel like an old fellow in Tennessee who made his
living by catching rattlesnakes. He caught one with
fourteen rattles and put it in a box with a glass top.
One day when he was sawing wood his little five-year-
old boy, Jim, took the lid off and the rattler wriggled
through and struck him in the cheek. He ran to his
father and said: "The rattler has bit me." The father
ran and chopped the rattler to pieces, and with his
jack-knife he cut a chunk from the boy's cheek and
then sucked and sucked at the wound to draw out the
poison. He looked at little Jim, watched the pupils
of his eyes dilate and watched him swell to three times
his normal size, watched his lips become parched and
cracked and his eyes roll and little Jim gasped and
died.

The father took him in his arms, carried him over to the side of the rattler, got on his knees and said: "Oh, God, I would not give little Jim for all the rattlers that ever crawled over the Blue Ridge Mountains."

And I would not give one boy for every dirty dollar you get from the hell-soaked liquor business or from every brewery and distiller this side of hell.

Listen! In a Northwest city a preacher sat at his breakfast table one Sunday morning. The doorbell rang, he answered it and there stood a little boy, 12 years of age. He was on crutches, right leg off at the knee, shivering, and he said, "Please, sir, will you come up to the jail and talk and plead with papa? He murdered mamma. Papa was good and kind but whisky did it, and I have to support my three little sisters. I sell newspapers and black boots. Will you go up and talk and pray with papa? And will you come home and be with us when they bring him back? The governor says we can have his body after they hang him."

The preacher was at the little hut when up drove the undertaker's wagon and they carried out the pine coffin. They led the little boy up to the coffin, he leaned over and kissed his father and sobbed, and said to his sisters: "Come on, sisters, kiss papa's cheeks before they grow cold." And the little, hungry, ragged whisky orphans hurried to the coffin, shrieking in agony. Police, whose hearts were adamant, buried their faces in their hands and rushed from the house, and the preacher fell on his knees and lifted his clenched fist and tear-stained face and took an oath before God and before the whisky orphans, that he would fight the cussed business until the undertaker carried him out in a coffin.

You men have a chance to show your manhood.

Then in the name of your pure mother, in the name of your manhood, in the name of your wife and the pure, innocent childrn that climb up in your lap and put their arms around your neck, in the name of all that is good and noble, fight the curse. Shall you men, who hold in your hands the ballot, and in that ballot hold destiny of womanhood, and children and manhood, shall you, the sovereign power, refuse to rally in the name of the defenseless men and women and native land? No.

I want every man to say: "God, you can count on me to protect my wife, and home, my mother and my children and the manhood of America."

By the mercy of God, which has given to you the unshaken and unshakable confidence of her you love. I beseech you to make a fight for the women who wait until the saloons spew out the husbands and their sons, and send them home, maudlin, brutish, devilish, stinking, bleary-eyed, bloated-faced drunkards.

BIBLIOGRAPHY

A. Books

Brown, Elijah P. *The Real Billy Sunday* New York: Fleming H. Revell Company, 1914.

Davis, Mac. *Baseball's Unforgettables.* New York: Bantam, 1966.

Ellis, William T. *Billy Sunday, The Man and His Message.* Chicago, Illinois: John C. Winston Company, 1936.

_____. *Billy Sunday, The Man and His Message.* Chicago: Moody Press, 1959.

Hall, Gordon Langley. *The Sawdust Trail.* Philadelphia: Macrae Smith Company, 1964.

Lockerbie, D. Bruce. *Billy Sunday.* Waco, Texas: Word Books, 1965.

McLoughlin, William G. *Billy Sunday Was His Real Name.* Chicago, Illinois: University of Chicago Press, 1955.

Rodeheaver, Homer. *Twenty Years With Billy Sunday.* Nashville: Cokesbury Press, 1936.

Smith, Robert. *Baseball.* New York: Simon and Schuster, 1947.

Thomas, Lee. *Billy Sunday.* Van Nuys: Bible Voice, 1974.

Thomas, Lee. *The Billy Sunday Story.* Grand Rapids, Michigan: Zondervan Publishing House, 1961.

Thonsson, Lester, A. Craig Baird, and Waldo W. Braden. *Speech Criticism.* New York: The Ronald Press Company, 1970.

Timberlake, James H. *Prohibition and the Progressive Movement.* New York: Atheneum, 1970.

B. Periodicals

Barton, Bruce. "Billy Sunday—Baseball Evangelist,"
  Collier's, (June 23, 1913), p. 30.

"Billy Sunday's War on the Devil in New York,"
  Literary Digest, CVIII (January 27, 1934), p. 21.

"Billy Sunday Sympathetically Interpreted," *Current
  Opinion* (1914) pp. 369-370.

"Conversion and Life of Billy Sunday," *Sword of the
  Lord*, (Feburary 2, 1979), pp. 1, 11.

Denison, Lindsay. "The Reverend Billy Sunday and
  His War on the Devil, " *American Magazine*,
  LXIV (September, 1907), pp. 450-469.

"Making Religion Yellow," *Nation*, XCII (June 11,
  1908), pp. 527-528.

"The Problem of Billy Sunday," *Literary Digest*,
  XLVII (June 14, 1913), pp. 1336-1337.

"A Revivalist Judged By Results," Outlook (April 11,
  1914), pp. 804-805.

C. Unpublished Materials

LaPanta, Gregory John. "An Analysis of the Use of
  Emotional Appeal in Selected Sermons of Billy
  Sunday," Unpublished Master's Thesis,
  Mankato, Minnesota, 1967.

D. Recorded Materials

"Yesterday's Voices," Word Records, Incorporated,
  Waco, Texas.

INDEX

SOWERS SERIES

ATHLETE
Billy Sunday, Home Run to Heaven
  by Robert Allen

EXPLORERS AND PIONEERS
Christopher Columbus, Adventurer of Faith and Courage
  by Bennie Rhodes
Johnny Appleseed, God's Faithful Planter, John Chapman
  by David Collins

HOMEMAKERS
Abigail Adams, First Lady of Faith and Courage
  by Evelyn Witter
Susanna Wesley, Mother of John and Charles
  by Charles Ludwig

HUMANITARIANS
Florence Nightingale, God's Servant at the Battlefield
  by David Collins
Teresa of Calcutta, Serving the Poorest of the Poor
  by D. Jeanene Watson

MUSICIANS AND POETS
Francis Scott Key, God's Courageous Composer
  by David Collins
Samuel Francis Smith, My Country, 'Tis of Thee
  by Marguerite E. Fitch